ALL THE WAY THE LORD HAS LED US

Dear Stilwells:
We are so grateful
for your family! Your
love & support on this
journey have meant
so much to us. Thank
you for everything!
Love & prayers,
Joni

Dedication

To my Lord and Savior, Jesus Christ, Who gave everything for me,

Thank You for all the way You have led us. I love You!

All the Way the Lord Has Led Us © 2016 Joan Elizabeth Moede
ISBN 13: 978-1540377128
ISBN 10: 1540377121

Special thanks to Dr. KJ Gilchrist and John Desaulniers, Jr. for their wisdom and help in publishing this book.

Cover and interior design by Sadie Desaulniers, www.manifoldgrace.com.

All photos courtesy of the author.

The author does not necessarily agree with all views of quoted authors, sources, or websites.

All reasonable attempts have been made to secure permission for copyrighted materials referenced.

Contents

Acknowledgements

To my husband, Paul, thank you for being a faithful man of God, for leading our son to the Lord and discipling him. Being your wife is a blessing and I am so thankful we have stood together through these storms. I love you!

To our extended family, thank you for going above and beyond the call of duty during this journey. We love each of you!

To the Body of Christ, how beautiful you are! Thank you for all the ways you have used your gifts, talents, treasures, passions, time and prayers to bless our family. Thank you to those who over many years, taught the Word of God to us, who mentored us and poured into our lives. We have been blessed by your reflection of His love!

To Pastor DeFord and all those at Bethany, and to Pastor Weaver and all those at New Hope who have walked with us through these difficulties, we are eternally grateful for the outpouring of love, prayers and support! We love you!

Preface

This book tells of our son's diagnosis of brain cancer and passing from this life less than a year later.

This book is also a testimony of how all the way the Lord has led us (Deuteronomy 8:2). It is a combination of Michael's Caring Bridge log, my personal journal and my thoughts since Michael's passing. There are also quotes from books I have read that have been a guide in the fog of this journey.

Through all of the decisions made, we included Michael in the decision making and we tried to respect his wishes.

I have tried to honestly share some of the challenges and decisions we as a family struggled with during Michael's illness. Some things I did not share in order to protect Michael's dignity. But I shared many things that I wish we had known and things which we learned along the way. It is my hope that they will be a help to those walking a similar road.

Paul and I were not perfect parents, nor was Michael the perfect child. We are sinners who have struggled daily with sinful natures. If we have done anything right, it is by God's grace and amazing mentors who helped us.

Reflecting back now, I can see how God faithfully prepared Paul, Michael and me for this road and carried us through. And as painful as it has been at times, I can truly say, "The Lord is good to all and His tender mercies are over all His works" (Psalm 145:9).

Joni Moede

February 2014

You can watch Michael's message at www.michaelsfinalmessage.com.

Introduction

Before reading this book, it might be helpful for you to understand my worldview. Around my seventeenth birthday, I became very aware that I was heading down a very treacherous path in my life. I knew I was a sinner and I knew that Jesus Christ came as God in the flesh and had lived the perfect sinless life, so that He could die on the cross for my sin. He conquered sin and death by rising from the dead. When I acknowledged my sin and asked Him to forgive me and be my Lord and Savior, He changed my life and my heart. His Holy Spirit now lives in me and I am no longer afraid of death because I have the assurance that I have eternal life with God in Heaven when I pass from this life.

I also view God as sovereign and good. He has allowed each of us free will. We can choose to go our own way, or we can choose to follow Him and allow Him to direct our lives. Yes, there is much evil, death and destruction in this world. But originally, this was not God's plan. His promise though is "that all things work together for good to those who love God, to those who are the called according to His purpose." (Romans 8:28). And best of all, Jesus Christ has gone to prepare a place for us, where there will be no more death or sorrow or evil.

Paul and I were married January 26, 1991. He was forty and I was close to turning thirty-three. Seven years later on May 13, 1998, Michael was born. Our first and only child. Much prayer had brought this child into the world. He was a true gift from God. I had put my job as a counselor on hold after he was born, because we wanted him to be at home with me. Financially this was a challenge, but well worth the sacrifices. When Michael was two, the Lord impressed on Paul's heart and mine that we should homeschool him. We are so thankful that we obeyed what He impressed on our hearts. There were many challenges, but so many more blessings! Because we had so much time with Michael growing up, we have wonderful memories. We also had so many opportunities to impress the Word of God on his heart. We see some of the fruit of those seeds planted and we are aware now more than ever that we reap what we sow (Galatians 6:7). God's Word does not return void (Isaiah 55:11).

The fall of 2010 was Michael's seventh-grade year. Paul was finishing our house so we could move in before winter. We had been living in a mobile home on our acreage for seventeen years. He had spent the last seven building our house, part-time, with Michael's help.

We enjoyed our first Thanksgiving in our new home. And it was a very special Christmas for us that year. The week of Christmas, Michael shot his first deer in our hay field. He was so excited! Christmas Eve, Paul's family came. It was a wonderful evening. We had a crackling fire in our fireplace and a Christmas tree that Paul and Michael had cut on our farm. After dinner, I lit the candles of our advent wreath and Paul read from the Bible, the Christmas story. Then Michael, who had been practicing and practicing on the piano, played "Carol of the Bells." I remember feeling so blessed! The Christmas before Michael was diagnosed was so special. But our lives were about to change drastically.

Peace I leave with you, My peace I give to you; not as the world gives do I give to you. Let not your heart be troubled, neither let it be afraid.

JOHN 14:27

CHAPTER ONE

The Diagnosis

Journal—Wednesday, February 2, 2011

Heard teaching yesterday about being in the desert and about seeking after other things and people instead of pursuing God. I feel this way. I want to pray more and be more faithful in pursuing God. I'm in the desert. I need to seek the Lord. Lord, help me to run after You, pursue You, go deeper in You. Give me a heart that loves You the way You deserve to be loved.

Insight Now

My journey through life can change in an instant. The desert can become an oasis or vice versa. I need to be thankful for the routine, ordinary days. They are days of preparation for the challenging days around the corner. I need to be thankful for the challenging days. They test me and show me God's faithfulness and strength and give me a clearer picture of Him. But whatever kind of day it is, I need to live it with Jesus by my side or should I say me by His side, living it out with Him, knowing that He sees the whole picture. He knows what is ahead for me, and I can hold on to His hand each step of the way. That is how my life is meant to be lived out—in communion with Him. After all, who loves me more than He who died for me?

Journal—Tuesday, March 1, 2011

Yesterday I took Michael to the doctor about his foot. He was perplexed as to why he has "drop foot" but no pain. He referred us to a neurologist. The neurologist tested Michael and has ordered an MRI on his brain. I have already thought through extremes. Read "The Lord is gracious and full of compassion, slow to anger and great in mercy. The Lord is good to all, and His tender mercies are over all His works. All Your works shall praise You, O Lord, and Your saints shall bless You" (Psalm 145:8-10).

Impressed to worship God through this time and to trust Him. Don't seek sympathy from others or charge God with wrong. Uphold God's character of good and merciful. Set the right tone in the home.

Insight Now

Looking back now, I am amazed at God's grace to us at this time. For over twenty years, Paul and I had listened to a radio program called *Searchlight.*[1] The pastor taught through the Bible, but also on the goodness and sovereignty of God. He knew of what he spoke; his wife was taken to Heaven after a car accident, leaving him with three small children. Then, years later his daughter was taken to Heaven in a similar car accident. Again and again we were reminded that when difficulties happen, look at the cross. Romans 5:8 states, "But God demonstrates His own love toward us, in that while we were still sinners, Christ died for us." And John 3:16 states, "For God so loved the world that He gave His only begotten Son, that whoever believes in Him should not perish but have everlasting life." Even though I may not understand all the whys, I can trust God through all these things that happen in my life and in the lives of those I love, because He has already shown me how much He loves and cares for me.

Journal—Friday, March 4, 2011

The devotional, *Joy and Strength*, is very good in light of all this today:

"Surely, He hath borne our griefs, and carried our sorrows" (Isaiah 53:4, KJV).

The way to think of God so as to know Him, is to think of Christ. Then we see Him, and can understand how tender and merciful and good He is. We see that if He sends us sorrows and difficulties, He only sends them because they are the true blessings, the things that are truly good. He would have us like Himself, with a happiness like His own, and nothing below it; and so as His own happiness is in taking sorrow and infirmity, and ever assisting, and giving and sacrificing Himself, He gives us sorrows too, and weaknesses, which are not the evils that we think them, but are what we should be most happy in, if we were perfect and had knowledge like Him. So there is a use and a service in all we bear, in all we do, which we do not know, but which He knows, and which in Christ He shows to us. It is a use for others, a hidden use, but one which makes all our life rich, and that richest which is most like Christ's.[2]

Doctor appointment today. MRI to look at Michael's brain. Paul more emotional, me less—usually the opposite. Both of us feel as if we have been kicked in the stomach—constant unsettling feeling that does not go away. [In fact, it lasted for days.] We are both praying and fasting Friday, Saturday and Sunday.

Journal—Saturday, March 5, 2011

The doctor called and they want another MRI this afternoon with contrast. Later, Paul, Michael and I met with the doctor. Michael [twelve years old at this time] asked that we not keep things from him and that he would be included in the decisions made. After the MRI, the doctor showed the three of us a picture of a large tumor in Michael's brain. She stated the brain tissue was infiltrated by other tissue with tentacles in several places. We were all stunned by the size of this tumor. It was obvious that this was life threatening. She recommended a biopsy to find out if it is cancer and if so, how best to treat it. As the three of us walked out of the hospital on a cold, gray, cloudy day, my thought was, "We've lost him." Not anger, just profound sadness.

Flashback

From infancy, I would place Michael in his bed at night, and then pray over him Numbers 6:24-26. "The Lord bless you and keep you; The Lord make His face shine upon you, and be gracious to you; The Lord lift up His countenance upon you, and give you peace." I had watched a pastor pray this over his flock. Then I would hold my open hand out to the Lord and give Michael to the Lord. I had heard Elisabeth Elliot talk on the radio about offering up our children to the Lord, holding them with an open hand—they are His. And they are entrusted to us for only a short time. I did this repeatedly, at first with great trepidation. Ever so slowly, I was able to entrust Michael to the Lord. I believe this helped prepare me for this moment. Michael would not be "lost," he would be in Heaven with Jesus. But he would be taken from me, from us, sooner than we had ever expected.

For years, I had also prayed a prayer that I kept in my planner. It was written by Betty Scott Stam:

> Lord, I give up all my own plans and purposes, all my own desires and hopes, and accept Thy will for my life. I give myself, my life, my all utterly to Thee to be Thine forever. Fill me and seal me with Thy Holy Spirit. Use me as Thou wilt, send me where Thou wilt, work out Thy whole will in my life at any cost, now and forever.[3]

Betty Scott Stam and her husband were missionaries to China. In 1938, after being taken captive by Chinese rebels, they were beheaded. Their infant daughter was left alone. What courage, what sacrifice!

Insight Now

People have asked me if I was angry with God. I don't ever remember being angry with Him about Michael's illness. In the past, I had been angry with God at different times in my life, before I had a better understanding of His love and His sovereignty. The more I come to know Him and His heart of love, the easier it has become to accept life—the past and the present.

There is a story in the Bible of Joseph who was sold into slavery by his brothers. After years of difficulty and imprisonment, his brothers return to find Joseph forgiving them. He tells them, "But as for you, you meant evil against me; but God meant it for good." (Genesis 50:20). This reminds me that no matter what situations happen in my life, or who may intend evil against me, or even when I make bad choices, God is sovereign, and He has a plan. He knows ahead of time what I will face and He has my best interest at heart. And He promises to work it for good in my life now and in eternity. Sometimes I look at situations with my limited perspective and wonder why, but I know that He has an eternal perspective that is different from mine.

Journal—Saturday, March 5, 2011 (evening)

While I was cleaning up the kitchen, Michael was laying on the floor in front of the fireplace. [Our kitchen/dining area and living room are one room.] He was tearful and afraid. I went to him and told him how Jesus' disciples were also afraid on the night when Jesus told them He was going away. I read to him from John 14:1. "Let not your heart be troubled; you believe in God, believe also in Me." We talked about how even in difficulties, God wants us to trust Him and be at peace. I encouraged him to read the rest of the chapter, and then went back to finishing the dishes, praying all the while that God would speak to his heart. In a few minutes, Michael excitedly said, "Mom, listen to this!" He read aloud to me John 14:27 "Peace I leave with you, My peace I give to you; not as the world gives do I give to you. Let not your heart be troubled, neither let it be afraid."

Insight Now

God is so faithful to answer my prayers. When I don't know quite what to do or to say, and I turn to Him for help, He acts in ways that amaze me. God used that verse to give Michael courage and peace.

Not that he didn't face fear again, he did at times. But, he hung onto that verse and trusted God even when facing the difficulties. That verse became one of Michael's favorites during the last months of this life. He knew God impressed that verse on his heart to give him peace in the midst of the storm.

Journal—Sunday, March 6, 2011

We went to my aunt's church for early service because we wanted Michael prayed over and anointed with oil as stated in Mark 6:13 and James 5:14. It was a special time. During the worship, there was an invitation for prayer. Paul, Michael and I went forward. Family and friends gathered around Michael and prayed for him as the pastor anointed him with oil.

Then we went to our home church for our usual Sunday service. Upon entering, the pastor asked Paul and me if at the close of the service the elders and the church could pray over us. We were very thankful that they wanted to do this. After the sermon, they brought three chairs up front. Paul, Michael and I sat facing the congregation. The pastor and elders stood behind us and the rest of the people in the church made a big circle around the church and prayed for us. I looked up and saw the pastor's five-year-old son, just sobbing while he stood holding his mother's hand. My heart ached for him also. Then they sang "Blest Be the Tie that Binds." We felt very cared for.

Sunday afternoon I talked more with the doctor. I had more questions. She stated surgery was not an option because the tumor was extensive and surgery would do damage. She wants him to have a biopsy at the Mayo Clinic.

Journal—Monday, March 7, 2011

Woke up very early. Weeping, silently weeping, tears rolling down my cheeks. I got up and picked up my Bible praying, "Please God, speak to me. Tell me what this is about." I opened my Bible randomly. On the page was Hebrews 11. [Normally, I am reading through the Bible, and don't just randomly open it to read. Hebrews 11 is known as "the faith chapter" because it tells of the great men and women of the Old Testament who had faith in God.] My initial thought was maybe God was going to heal Michael. I started reading from verse one. When I came to verse five, I read about Enoch. God took him because He delighted in him. I stopped reading and God spoke very clearly to my heart, "I'm taking Michael because I delight in him." I knew this was from the Lord; it gave me such peace. It was a bittersweet moment.

Insight Now

I am so, so thankful God gently spoke those words to my heart! As a mom, I would be wondering what I did wrong. Was I a really bad mom? Did I not give him enough good food? Did I give him too much bad food? Hadn't I nursed him for a year and a half when he was first born? Wasn't my dad in his eighties and still doing well after all the years of not the healthiest lifestyle? What God spoke to me silenced all those questions and continues to do so to this day, even when I have doubts.

Caring Bridge Log Monday, March 7, 2011

On March 4th and 5th Michael had two MRI's indicating his brain tissue is being infiltrated by some other tissue. A biopsy was recommended. We are awaiting the doctor's call as to where this will be conducted and when. Please pray for courage for our family.

We are thankful for all the prayers and support from our extended families, our church, and friends. In the midst of this storm, we are remembering that Jesus is with us. Psalm 145:9 "His tender mercies are over all His works!"

Journal—Monday, March 7, 2011 (Evening)

Met with a friend who has been down this road. Her suggestions were very helpful. Take a trip and make some memories. Take lots of pictures.

Caring Bridge Log—Wednesday, March 9, 2011

Michael is still scheduled to go to the Mayo clinic next week. At this point we are not sure which day, but tentatively Thursday, March 17. They will do tests this day and possibly a biopsy of his brain on Friday, March 18.

We have special plans for Michael this weekend. We appreciate all your prayers and support.

Caring Bridge Log—Wednesday, March 16, 2011

Thanks to all of you for all your prayers, encouragement and support during this time. It has been such a blessing to read your notes!

We had a wonderful weekend at Disney World in Florida (courtesy of my dad!). It was a much needed diversion for all of us, but especially for Michael and great family time. Hopefully, I will figure out how to post some of the pictures tomorrow.

We arrived near Rochester tonight and are staying with a very gracious family who open their home to people in need. My sister and her husband are with us here and have been a great help. God truly supplies all that we need. Although this is a difficult time in our journey, we have a peace that passes understanding.

Tomorrow we will meet with the doctor and will find out what tests will be completed. My sister brought her laptop, so I will try to update more often.

The verse on my mind this morning when I awoke was Joshua 1:9 "Be strong and of good courage; do not be afraid nor be dismayed, for the Lord your God is with you wherever you go." Michael memorized this verse when he was about three or four years old.

Caring Bridge Log—Thursday, March 17, 2011

Thank you for all your prayers today! We needed them. We met with two neurologists today, a social worker, went to an educational class about surgery, and Michael had another MRI. We have to be at the hospital at 9:00 a.m. tomorrow for the biopsy, which should take place sometime after 10:00 a.m.

Please pray for courage for all of us. And Michael asks that we pray that all goes well, that God would guide the surgeon's hands, and that he would not be sick from the anesthesia. We will be updating as soon as the surgery is over.

Caring Bridge Log—Friday, March 18, 2011

They just informed us that the biopsy samples have been taken and they are closing him up. We will not know the results for several days.

Please pray for a speedy recovery with no complications—especially no seizures. Thank you for all your prayers!

Caring Bridge Log—Friday, March 18, 2011

Thank you, thank you, thank you for all your prayers! Michael is recovering in the ICU. We met with the doctor and all went well. Hopefully, Michael will be discharged tomorrow or the day after and we can return home. We will wait to hear from our doctor in Des Moines who will receive the report on the biopsy.

At this time, Michael is awake, has eaten some ice chips and a little ginger ale. He seems to be his normal self except for feeling a little groggy.

Caring Bridge Log—Saturday, March 19, 2011

Michael has slept well all night and was able to walk two laps around the ICU before going to bed. We feel so blessed that he is doing so well. Thank you again for praying for him.

Caring Bridge Log—Sunday, March 20, 2011

Michael was discharged Saturday and we returned yesterday about 5:30 p.m. Then we all slept in today! Much needed rest. Paul is fighting a cold. But, Michael is doing well. He had a little bit of a headache last night but today is doing better. We are hoping to have a quiet week. I will update again when we hear about the results of the biopsy.

Thank you again for all your notes of encouragement, prayers and calls. I printed off a copy of all your notes on Caring Bridge so Michael can have them. If you have called and I have not returned your call, my apologies. I am just slow at getting regrouped! Please know we appreciate all the support!

"For My thoughts are not your thoughts,

Nor are your ways My ways," says the Lord.

"For as the heavens are higher than the earth,

So are My ways higher than your ways,

And My thoughts than your thoughts."

ISAIAH 55:8-9

CHAPTER TWO

The Prognosis

Caring Bridge Log—Tuesday, March 22, 2011

Our doctor here talked to the Mayo doctor today. She reported to us that Michael has grade three (on a scale of 1 to 4) astrocytoma, another name is glioma. She is going to meet with us tomorrow morning to talk about treatment options. We will update our journal as we learn more.

Please pray for us for wisdom and courage. We feel like we are being carried along by God's grace.

Caring Bridge Log—Wednesday, March 23, 2011

Our day was full of God's grace! After dropping Michael off to be with a gracious family, Paul and I went to meet with the doctor. On the way up to her office, God arranged to have a dear friend meet us, who truly just happened to be passing by. She gave me a hug and words of encouragement. What a blessing! Then we met with our doctor, who was extremely gracious and we are so thankful for her.

She told us with chemo and radiation Michael would probably be back for treatment in about six months because the cancer would shrink but would not be completely gone. His life expectancy would be less than a year, but his quality of life would be greatly diminished.

Without treatment, he would have about six months to live. Paul and I have chosen to try natural treatments and not go the chemo/radiation route because of the side effects and little gain. Our doctor was very respectful of our decision and said she would be available to help us if we need any medication later for pain management. She is hooking us up with a physical therapist to help Michael with his drop foot problem.

We told Michael all of this and he, as usual, handled it very courageously. He has asked all along that we not keep anything from him.

Paul and I are very, very grateful for all the prayers and support. We still pray for healing and that if possible this cup would pass from us, but His will and not ours be done.

Flashback

When Michael was about to turn nine or ten, I asked him a question. We were on our gravel road coming home. I looked in the rearview mirror.

"What do you want for your birthday?" I asked.

He thought and then said "I want to go to Heaven."

Stunned, I said, "You want to go to Heaven? Well, that is not up to me. Only God decides that."

He then explained why he wanted to go there. We had been listening to someone teach about Heaven from the book of Revelation. He knew Heaven was going to be a special place!

My next question, "So, what else do you want for your birthday?"

Journal—Wednesday, March 23, 2011

[I bought a new journal that had verses from Psalms in it. This is what I wrote on the first page]:

A good place to start this part of our journey—with praise. Thank you, Lord, for the gift of Michael! I praise You for Your mercy and goodness and that You have a plan for us, for good and not for evil, to give us a "future and a hope" (Jeremiah 29:11, NLT).

Reading today in Deuteronomy 8:16 "Who fed you in the wilderness with manna, which your fathers did not know, that He might humble you and that He might test you, to do you good in the end." Paul has said he feels this is a test like Job's.

Journal—Friday, March 25, 2011

Michael played games with friends at church today and the ladies took time to pray with me. Was very good.

Joy and Strength this morning challenged me. It was about Mary, the mother of Jesus, it says:

"Behold the handmaid of the Lord; be it unto me according to thy word" (Luke 1:38, KJV).

We can see plainly how her ready self-surrender in faith, in trust, to her unknown, her mysterious destiny; how her instant expression of entire self-oblation to the Divine Will, to all that she was called to be and to do, to bear all that might in the future be required of her, is a constant witness of the mind that ought to animate and pervade the whole action of the soul. Life, if true, should be always the offering up of what we are, to do our best for Him who has called us. The responsibilities, the ventures, the conscious obligations which press on the soul, with all their condition and unknown possibilities, supply the question that is to be solved; but the true response is the result of a habit formed through countless, nameless acts of conscientious obedience, which by use have become the bright and cheerful exercise of the one purpose of giving its best and purest to One most fully loved.[4]

Insight Now

Throughout the Bible are people that inspire me as well as warn me. Mary is such an inspiration of surrender to God. Her future and her Son's were unknown and yet she trusted—even when told, "a sword will pierce through your own soul also" (Luke 2:35). Those words have echoed through my mind many a time after having a child. Loving a child leaves a parent so vulnerable.

Around this time my dear friend, Kim, had a dream about Paul, Michael and me. This is what she wrote to me:

> In my dream, you and Paul and Michael were sitting in a huge Hand, which I somehow knew was God's Hand. Around the Hand it was brightly lit and I could see a bit of the arm and a white robe on the arm. All three of you looked at peace and content. I just felt clearly that the Lord was saying that He is taking care of the three of you. I know that YOU know that, but it just gave me such a peace and assurance to be reminded that the three of you are indeed in the Lord's Hands.

Acceptance of God's sovereignty brings such peace to my heart when I am troubled. There is no situation that catches Him off guard.

No situation that surprises Him. He is omniscient (all-knowing), omnipotent (all powerful), and omnipresent (everywhere at once). But most importantly, He is love (I John 4:8).

Whereas you do not know what will happen

tomorrow. For what is your life? It is even a vapor

that appears for a little time and then vanishes away.

JAMES 4:14

CHAPTER THREE

Making Memories

Journal—Sunday, March 27, 2011

Woke up at 4:30 a.m. Struggling with balancing everything and all the demands on our time. Lord, help me know what is best.

Caring Bridge Log—Tuesday, March 29, 2011

Just a note to update you. We are still very thankful for all your prayers and encouragement during this time. We have received so much helpful information about treating Michael naturally. Thanks to all who have helped with this.

Please continue to pray for Michael and for our family. We need wisdom and guidance in the days ahead.

Yesterday we met with the people from Make-a-Wish. They are very helpful and are working on a plan! Please pray that God would orchestrate what is best. Thank you!

And please pray for me. I am feeling overwhelmed with life at the moment. Just the daily things that I am juggling. It's hard to determine priorities at times (doing things for Michael to help him, or spending time being with Michael).

God has faithfully been providing and encouraging us. We appreciate each of you and God bless you for all your prayers! I have heard it said, "Prayer is the most important work!"

Insight Now

There are so many decisions to make when someone has been diagnosed with cancer. The multitude of choices seem overwhelming at times. For us, it was of the utmost importance to be on the same page regarding our son. We prayed much about this. Paul felt impressed to try the natural approach—so we did.

Journal—Wednesday, March 30, 2011

Yesterday was a most difficult day. Paul has been in bed sick for two days. He is better today. I ran numerous errands, buying special food. Michael is struggling with feeling disappointed about his life being over so soon. I asked him what was the hardest part. He told me missing Paul and me and not being able to win more souls for Christ. What a heart!

Flashback

When Michael was about six years old, I read to him about George Whitefield from the book, *The Light and the Glory* by Peter Marshall and David Manuel. In talking about Whitefield preaching to the coal miners it says:

> Whitefield felt a deep burden for them, and as they had no church—indeed, had never heard a preacher—he resolved

to bring them the Gospel of Jesus Christ in the open air. Accordingly, he found some high ground, near the exit of the mines, and as they began to appear, he began to preach on the Sermon on the Mount. Before long, several hundred miners were standing before him, listening to his words about a Savior who came, not for the righteous but for sinners. He told them of Jesus' love for them--so great a love that He gave Himself over to His persecutors to be crucified, and that as the nails were driven into His hands and feet His only thought was for them--for each man standing there that day. And as they raised Him up, and He hung there hour after hour in unspeakable agony, He was suffering for them, that they might be forever freed from their sins. Because He loved them that much.

Suddenly, Whitefield noticed pale streaks forming on faces black with grime. . .[5]

After reading this to Michael, he got down on his knees and while sobbing, he begged God to use him to save souls. I was amazed at how God was working in his heart.

Insight Now

Deuteronomy 6:6–7 says, "And these words which I command you today shall be in your heart. You shall teach them diligently to your children, and shall talk of them when you sit in your house, when you walk by the way, when you lie down, and when you rise up."

This confirms to me how what we pour into the lives of our children bears much fruit. When Michael was two years old, we celebrated

Christmas using an advent wreath. It became a yearly tradition to help us focus on Christ during the holiday season. When Christmas was over, we continued having family devotions. I asked Paul if I could read some from a kid's devotional book after dinner. He was fine with it and in a short time took over reading the Bible to Michael and me and then leading us in prayer. At that time, our pastor and his wife, told of how their family put a map of the world on the wall and how they prayed over the nations during the week.[6] So, on the wall above our kitchen table, we put a map of the world. This helped Michael learn geography as well as the importance of world missions. Eventually, our family devotional time looked like this:

Paul would read a portion of the Bible.

We would recite Bible verses we were memorizing.

We would pray over the people on the continent of that day and any missionaries we knew of in those areas:

Sunday—North America

Monday—Central and South America

Tuesday—Europe and Russia

Wednesday—Africa

Thursday—The Middle East

Friday—India, China, and the rest of Asia

Saturday—Australia, New Zealand, Indonesia, and the surrounding islands.

We would sing a hymn or Bible song.

The benefits of family devotional time are eternal! Michael memorized so much scripture, just by reviewing a few verses at a time on a daily basis. He was able to memorize chapters of the Bible. His understanding of the Bible and God's heart for him also grew. Not that we had all the answers, we were learning too. But we discussed questions that came up and learned where to look for answers we did not know. Having a set time for family devotions, after dinner, while we were all still at the table was beneficial too. It was part of our routine, not out of legalism, but a choice, a priority, to continue growing in grace and the knowledge of God.

Journal—Thursday, March 31, 2011

A friend came with her boys. We cleaned, they played games in the loft. We had a good prayer time. Her boys struggling with Michael's illness. Lord, help us to know how to handle this.

Journal—Sunday, April 3, 2011

Days fly by. Went to my brother's house last night for dinner. They were very, very gracious and love Michael! (They had fresh lobster flown in from Maine and then cooked them! WOW!)

Many people still calling and offering to help. Still feeling there are so many things I need to do. Lord, please give me grace and strength to plan and do all this. Please orchestrate our Make-A-Wish trip according to Your will.

Journal—Monday, April 4, 2011

Paul and I thought about canceling the Make-A-Wish trip last night, but this morning read about having faith and not fear. Hebrews 13:6 (AMP) says: "So we take comfort and are encouraged and confidently and boldly say, The Lord is my Helper; I will not be seized with alarm [I will not fear or dread or be terrified]. What can man do to me?"

Deuteronomy 31:8 "And the Lord, He is the One who goes before you. He will be with you, He will not leave you nor forsake you; do not fear nor be dismayed."

Isaiah 41:10 "Fear not, for I am with you; be not dismayed, for I am your God. I will strengthen you, yes, I will help you, I will uphold you with My righteous right hand."

Journal—Thursday, April 7, 2011

God is so amazing! I am in awe of what God is doing. He does way above and beyond all that we ask or think! [Regarding the RV trip.]

Insight Now

Originally, Michael wanted to go to Israel with his favorite Bible teacher for his Make-A-Wish trip. But they were not traveling there at that time. His next choice was to take an RV trip out west and see the redwood trees. When I told him this was near his favorite Bible teacher's church, he wanted to go there too! So, after contacting the church, it was arranged. Paul and I were blessed by this opportunity. After listening to this pastor on the radio for over twenty years, we had always wanted to visit his church. God brings great blessings in the midst of our great trials.

Caring Bridge Log—Friday, April 8, 2011

We are so thankful for all of you! We have been blessed reading the Caring Bridge guestbook and reading the cards you have mailed. I wish I could respond to each one personally.

Last week Michael was fitted for a brace that helps his foot not drop so much when he walks. He wears it every day. He has had to make many adjustments but is accepting them well. He is not experiencing any pain and still has his great sense of humor. He keeps Paul and me laughing many times each day!

Thanks to those who have offered to help in so many ways. We appreciate each one of you. Thank you especially for all your prayers. The love of God through the body of Christ is amazing to us! God bless each of you!

Insight Now

How many times have I been a turtle? Hearing of someone's difficulty or need, but pulling my head into my shell and withdrawing for different reasons, at different times. Sometimes because I don't know what to do, or I'm too busy, or I want to protect myself. How many times have I not responded out of fear of what other people will think, which is my pride? How many times have I been selfish, because reaching out wasn't convenient. And sometimes, there are so many needs, I think I can't do everything!

After walking through this season, my heart far more frequently wants to help when I hear of others in need, because I now know what it is like to hurt deeply. Silence at times can be deafening. I don't want to be silent any longer. Now, when I hear of a need, when someone is hurting, I try to ask the Lord how He wants me to respond. Should I pray, take a meal, send a note, give financially or just be there to listen? When I do what He impresses on my heart, I am truly blessed. "It is more blessed to give than to receive" (Acts 20:35). And I don't have to feel guilty because I don't have to do everything, I just have to do what the Lord wants me to do. He is the Head of the Body of Christ and He orchestrates each member. He is like an orchestra conductor telling each orchestra member with their different talents, when to play their part, and how to play their piece of music. And when we let Him lead, it brings forth a beautiful sound that is in harmony and blesses many.

Journal—Sunday, April 10, 2011

The Lord has been impressing on my heart Isaiah 10:15 (NLT) "Can the ax boast greater power than the person who uses it? Is the saw greater than the person who saws? Can a rod strike unless a hand is moving it? Can a cane walk by itself?" Yielded to be wielded. God wants me to yield my heart, my life, my pain to Him so He can wield it for His glory. We are the tools, He is the hand that uses them in His way, His time, for His purposes and His glory.

Insight Now

The people who have ministered to me the most, are those who have been through very painful events, circumstances and losses but have not become bitter. They have lived out their faith loving God and loving others—a simple childlike trust that their Heavenly Father will work for good any evil, any injustice, any loss, and that He is able to do above and beyond all that we ask or think. They can trust Him because they know His heart, and they came to this understanding by day in and day out reading and studying His Word—speaking to Him and letting Him speak to them.

Journal—Monday, April 18, 2011

Leaving Oregon—a piece of Heaven. So hard to leave. Such a beautiful state and the fellowship! God give me grace to go forward. Need to find ways to serve. Keep eyes on the Lord. Live before the face of God.

Insight Now

The Make-A-Wish trip was such a blessing! Friday, April 15, was a day of prayer and fasting for Michael, organized by a dear friend. It was also the day we arrived at the California redwoods. That day was so special! It was cloudy and a light misty rain was falling. While we walked in the forest of tall trees, I felt as if Heaven were weeping, knowing we were on a final journey.

We spent the night in an RV park called the Emerald Forest, which rightly describes our being parked amid the giant trees. In the morning we visited Patrick's Point to see the ocean. Of course, being from Iowa the ocean is very special to us because we rarely see it! So, we spent several hours on the beach picking up shells, driftwood and fossils. Michael also found several strange white rocks that had clear parts in them. We realized later these were agates.

We then headed for Oregon. Looking back, that was a very healing place to visit. Just to gently worship the Lord, and to be in His presence can be like a soothing balm in the wound. To partake of communion and to truly "taste and see that the Lord is good" (Psalm 34:8). To be reminded of how much He loves us, cares for us and is with us in the midst of our painful journey. I think of it now as how the hobbits in the movie, *The Lord of the Rings: The Fellowship of the Ring*, must have felt, entering Rivendell for the first time, awed by the beauty and loveliness of the place.[7] The safety, security and comfort made by so many who had sacrificed so much and worked so hard to establish it, not knowing at the time how it would be such a blessing to others, years and years later. Then, the hobbits having to depart such a haven, knowing they were headed for many difficulties down the road—wishing they could stay forever, knowing, however, it was not to be. But they were better prepared, and strengthened for their long journey ahead. Such a gratefulness in my heart for the blessing of that part of the body of Christ.

What am I pouring my life into now? Will it be a blessing for others? Will it matter in eternity? There are so many people hurting in this world. Is what I am doing, what He has for me? Is it His main purpose for me, or is it my plan? Am I doing it out of a grateful heart of love for Him? If so, it will be worth it; I won't regret it on the other side. The body of Christ, when functioning under His headship, is so awesome—and can accomplish such blessings and reflect His love so beautifully, if yielded to be wielded.

Caring Bridge Log—Monday, April 25, 2011

Michael chose to take an RV trip to the west coast to see the redwoods for his Make-A-Wish. We had a wonderful time as you can see in the photos. We also visited Oregon, the Grand Canyon, and Colorado Springs. Paul did a great job driving! We are so thankful for all the prayers! We felt we were carried along on angel wings!

Michael has noticed some changes. He looks sleepy because the muscles in his face aren't working like they use to. He also went to softball practice and realized he can't throw or hit as well as he was able to last year. But he is still able to walk and still beats Paul and me when playing Blokus. He is not in any pain.

Journal—Monday, May 2, 2011

Many unknowns ahead. I keep saying the name of Jesus over and over to stay close to Him—to stay in the present, not the past or in fears of the future.

Caring Bridge Log—Tuesday, May 3, 2011

What a blessing last night to see all my fellow homeschool moms and get so many hugs and words of encouragement! Thank you to all who are in those groups and who have been fasting and praying for us!!! We feel so thankful for the whole body of Christ.

Yesterday I picked up a used book about Jim Elliot, a missionary to South America. He was the husband of Elisabeth Elliot. He was killed by the Aucas in the 1950's. This morning Paul, Michael and I discussed this quote from his journal:

> As I read Job 12:10 again, "in His hand is the life of every living thing," I recognized that all I am and have is the Almighty's. He could in one instant change the whole course of my life—with accident, tragedy, or any event unforeseen. Job is a lesson in acceptance, not of blind resignation, but of believing acceptance, that what God does is well done. So, Father, with happy committal I give You my life again this morning—not for anything special, simply to let You know that I regard it as Yours. Do with it as it pleases You. Only give me great grace to

do for the glory of Christ Jesus whatever comes to me, 'in sickness and in health!'[8]

We discussed how we can only do this by looking at the cross and knowing He gave everything to make us His. How can I doubt His great love when faced with trials? All is bearable in His presence. He is truly in the fiery furnace with us! He prepared us beforehand and gives us His great grace in the midst of all. We hope this is as encouraging to you as it is to us.

Tonight, Michael has his second ballgame of the season. Last week he had three hits, which we were all happy about. A good friend ran the bases for him. We are thankful that he is able to play this year and are blessed by a very supportive team and coach.

The 13th of May is Michael's 13th birthday. Would you pray for that weekend? We have three parties planned (Paul's family, friends, and my family). It was Michael's wish to have separate parties. But we have many offers of help already so God will give more grace!

Journal—Wednesday, May 4, 2011

Need to keep a servant's heart. Give as unto Him. Need unity between Paul and I. Concerned enemy trying to divide us. I remember Elisabeth Elliot saying on the radio, "Love hardly notices when others do it wrong." Lord, fill me with your love as I walk through this. Read today in a commentary, "If you pray for one thing, ask the Lord to make you a man or woman of love!"[9]

Insight Now

After Michael passed, someone asked Paul and me how we got through this together. It was God's grace, the prayers of so many that to this day help us in so many ways, and praying together as a couple. Paul always prays over me every morning and every evening, as he did with Michael too. And I for him. But, when we begin to be at dire odds with each other, when things start to escalate, we are learning and have found that stopping and praying helps immensely—even if we have to stop and pray several times. Asking for God's intervention is humbling, but helps us regain perspective, remembering "be kind to one another, tenderhearted, forgiving one another, even as God in Christ forgave you" (Ephesians 4:32).

Journal—Saturday, May 7, 2011

I feel the weight of so much on me. Lord help me to cast all my care on You. Help me to serve You and them out of love and not count the cost. Please grant me a gentle and quiet spirit. When praying moments after I wrote this—these thoughts came to me. Not only does the ax not boast against Him who wields it, but it does not complain or think about how much it has to chop. It is the Lord's work. He expends the energy. I am the tool He uses. His grace is sufficient for me, for His strength is made perfect in weakness, (II Corinthians 12:9). The ax does not tire—I need to rest in Him. Find rest in His yoke. "Come to Me, all you who labor and are heavy laden, and I will give you rest. Take My yoke upon you and learn from Me, for I am gentle and lowly in heart, and you will find rest for your souls. For My yoke is easy and My burden is light" (Matthew 11:28-30).

Journal—Monday, May 9, 2011

Have been struggling with wishing I were somewhere else, some place beautiful. Realizing it is God and His presence I long for. Need to stay in the present, giving thanks for all I do have.

Caring Bridge Log—Tuesday, May 10, 2011

Thanks to everyone for your continued support, cards, offers to help and most importantly your prayers! We had a very nice Mother's Day. Paul and Michael both bought me beautiful cards and a gift. My mom, my sister and her husband came for dinner. We had a great time.

Michael is hoping to go to the ballgame tonight. It is suppose to be over 90 degrees this afternoon. Last week he had a hit but struck out once. He enjoys playing with the team.

He still has no pain and no seizures which we are thankful for. Thanks again for all your prayers. God has wonderfully provided support through all of you! God Bless Each of You!!!

Flashback

On the way home from church that Sunday, I opened a gift bag from someone I had not met, but whose son was already in Heaven. Her heart had hurt for mine on that Mother's Day. She sent a clear plaque with scripture verses about trusting in the Lord. Tiny pink roses were at the base. Also in the bag were some chocolates--how did she know? And a book of God's promises. Her card was so caring. What kindness from someone who just wanted to bless me on Mother's Day. This was so sweet a reflection of God's love!

Caring Bridge Log—Wednesday, May 11, 2011

We would so appreciate your prayers for our family. Last night I started feeling sick and I want to be healthy for Michael's party this weekend. I think I am just run down.

Would you also pray for good weather for his parties this weekend. We have some outdoor activities planned and are hoping for no rain and nice weather.

Michael didn't participate in the game last night because of the ninety-five degree heat.

Thank you again for your continued prayers. It is such a comfort to know we can posts these requests and know you will be praying.

Journal—Saturday, May 14, 2011

Yesterday was Michael's 13th birthday. Was a good day. I was tearful. He is so special. Today is his party at church. Lord grant me grace, strength, love, and humility.

Flashback

For Michael's birthday party at the church, we wanted a banner with a scripture verse on it. Michael chose Daniel 12:3 (NIV), "Those who are wise will shine like the brightness of the heavens, and those who lead many to righteousness, like the stars for ever and ever." The year before, he had chosen this verse to go with the knight's shield he had designed while studying the Middle Ages. The shield had a bright shining star on it with this verse underneath.

During that time we had read *Sir Knight of the Splendid Way* by W.E. Cule. This is a quote describing how the book,

> ...depicts life as a journey, reaching toward a beacon of hope in the City of the Great King. Beckoned by the King to travel the Splendid Way, the young knight must keep

his armor on at all costs. All along the way he is tempted to take his armor off. Many try to convince him that the battle is not worth the fight. But only those who keep their armor on can see the real battle that rages, and only those with pure hearts will see the King. . . Carry the Emblem of the King, a light in the darkest battle, a healing salve for the wounded, and a beacon of hope for the weak and forlorn. Be strong and courageous as you contend with the Black Knight; be heartened and reassured when you behold the Vision of the Face—tender, resplendent, and filled with immeasurable love![10]

Caring Bridge Log—Monday, May 16, 2011

Thanks to each of you who posted notes, or sent cards, or prayed! Michael read each one and was very touched! God answers prayer!!! Michael had a fantastic birthday weekend, thanks to each of you!

Friday, the Park and Recreation Department put together a huge envelope full of cards (more than we could count!) for Michael. Paul's coworkers brought this over and it was a great blessing to our son. Thanks to all of you who work with Paul and took the time to do this.

Friday night Paul's family blessed Michael with a fish-fry potluck. It was good to see everyone. Special thanks to Uncle Dave for catching and cooking all the fish, and to Kenton and Jenny for hosting the party. We all had a great time.

Saturday, we had Michael's party. Our Chinese student and many friends from church helped. Thank you, thank you, thank you to each one that helped! You blessed Michael and us so much! It was a wonderful time and God answered our prayers and held off the rain so the kids could be outside playing games. We were blessed by each family that came and showed their love to Michael. Paul and I felt so encouraged and strengthened. It was so good to see and visit with those we had not seen for awhile. I will try to post some pictures later.

On Sunday after church, we went to the Junior Duck Stamp award ceremony. We are so proud of Michael and the great job that he did on his picture!

Then Sunday evening my family came to dinner and we played games. We had a great time. Michael is still doing well at playing chess! My mom loves to play dominoes so we had a fun game of that also.

Thanks for all your prayers! We again felt like we were being carried along through this. Michael wanted me to specifically say, "Thank you to each one!" God again blessed us through friends and family. The love of God through the body of Christ is amazing! God Bless Each of You!

Caring Bridge Log—Saturday, May 21, 2011

Last night was Michael's piano recital. Several young people and Michael all played for their families. It was a wonderful time! God answered our prayers again and helped each student play their best. We had told Michael that he didn't have to play if he did not want to, the decision was his. He knows that his right hand is not working like it used to and it is a struggle for him. But he allowed God to give him extra grace and we are so proud of him for being so courageous.

We talked about how God truly pours in the strength and courage right at the time we need it. He is so faithful!!!

A big thank you to his teacher. She is such an angel! She has worked so well with Michael and is so encouraging to all her students. What a blessing!

Journal—Monday, May 23, 2011

Reading about how God uses pain to refine our hearts.

> Silver is tried by fire and the heart by pain... But in the fire thou shalt not be burned; only thy dross shall be removed....

> The main end of our life is not to do, but to become. For this we are being moulded and disciplined each hour. You cannot understand why year after year the stern ordeal is perpetuated; you think the time is wasted; you are doing nothing. Yes, but you are situated in the set of circumstances that gives you the best opportunity for manifesting, and therefore acquiring, the qualities in which your character is naturally deficient. And the Refiner sits patiently beside the crucible, intent on the process, tempering the heat, and eager that the scum should pass off, and His own face become perfectly reflected in the surface.

> Only be satisfied... that nothing can befall thee but what has first passed concerning thee in the courts of heaven. And say with the saintly Fletcher: "I felt the will of my God like unto a soft pillow, upon which I could lie down and find rest and safety in all circumstances. Oh, it is a blessed thing to sink into the will of God in all things.

Absolute resignation to the Divine will baffles a thousand temptations; confidence in our Savior carries us sweetly through a thousand trials." [11]

I need to have hope and trust Him and thank Him in expectation of what He will do in Michael, Paul and me. Lord, please prepare us and plan what is best for us in the future. We need You and Your presence with us. We need Your guidance. Thank you, Lord! "He fashions their hearts individually; He considers all their works" (Psalm 33:15).

Journal—Tuesday, May 24, 2011

Softball last night. Michael had two hits. A friend ran the bases for him. Michael almost didn't go to the game. [During this time period, we began to notice that Michael would flip flop with his decisions, one minute wanting to go, the next minute wanting to stay—sometimes very emotional about it. We think this was associated with his brain tumor. They told us there would probably be personality changes.] I told him the team was expecting him. He went, had a good attitude, and was glad afterward.

Journal—Friday, May 27, 2011

We are all battling crankiness. I feel like such a failure at times. I fear what life will be like in the future without Michael. I feel the brunt of both their anger. I know much is my fault for not being "gentle and quiet." Lord, please help us! Grant us hearts of love and compassion.

Insight Now

When tension mounts at home, I can either escalate it or diffuse it by how I respond. The tone that I use is as important as the words that I choose. How many times have I just let loose and wounded those I love? Am I fighting with my family or for them? They are not the enemy and they need as much mercy and grace as I have been so freely given by my Lord. I cannot do this on my own. I need to choose to stop and pray, to choose to forgive, to ask their forgiveness and allow the Lord, by His Spirit to love through me. I do not have it in myself to love rightly. But as I choose to yield to Him, He answers my prayers and helps me. Favorite scriptures: "On her tongue is the law of kindness" (Proverbs 31:26). "A gracious woman retains honor" (Proverbs 11:16). "What is desired in a man is kindness" (Proverbs 19:22).

Journal—Sunday, May 29, 2011

Yesterday at friends' farm. Read a chapter entitled "Don't Jump Ship", from the book, *A Future and a Hope*. Was very good to read. The author talked about how in the storms of life we want to leave, jump ship. God wants us to wait on Him.[12] Not that I would leave Paul, we don't ever talk divorce. But my heart could shut down toward him and that would not be good. Felt impressed to not give up. Wait and see what God will do.

Caring Bridge Log—Friday, June 3, 2011

My friend just posted Michael's birthday pictures for us. Hope you enjoy them. We have been busy but all doing well. Michael had a fun day last weekend fishing at a very special farm pond. Thanks to all those who helped with that, especially Donnie and Nancy, and Aunt Katie and Uncle Ralph. (Uncle Ralph took Paul and Michael in the fishing boat trolling for fish—for hours!) They caught about twenty-seven and enjoyed eating some the next day. What a blessed time!

Tuesday night at softball, Michael got a hit and then helped in a doubleplay at second base. It was a good game.

Flashback

The day at the farm was so special! This gracious couple, friends of my aunt and uncle, had heard about Michael and wanted him to come for the day and fish. They and their friends, treated us like family, opening their home, blessing us abundantly with food, fellowship, fun and lots of hugs! Michael and Paul enjoyed fishing in their pond. A friend and I took a canoe out. I love being on the water. I visited with new friends and spent time resting on the swing by the pond with a good book to read. This convinces me I have much to learn about hospitality. It is so healing when caring people come alongside and show the love of Christ to hurting hearts!

Caring Bridge Log—Friday, June 10, 2011

Please continue to pray for Michael. This afternoon he had a mild seizure. This has been difficult and somewhat scary for all of us. The doctor is prescribing him some medication to help subdue mild seizure activity.

Flashback

About this time, I began to wonder, would Michael have a severe seizure that would end his life? We were told this was a possibility. Every time I left the house to run errands, I would wonder if he would be alive when I returned. I knew the Lord did not want me to live in fear. So, I would always be sure to leave on a good note. To let him know I loved him. And then pray for God's timing and asking if we could both be there when he passed. God was and always is faithful.

Caring Bridge Log—Monday, June 13, 2011

Thank you again for all your prayers for Michael. It is such a comfort to know that there are so many people praying for our family! Michael is doing well. He has not had any other seizures. Our doctor prescribed medication for him on Friday that will subdue any minor seizures. Friends of our use this same medication with their son who has had a brain injury. It was so nice to know they thought this was a very helpful medication with little side effects.

We had hoped to attend the Friday evening session of the homeschool conference, but thought it best to stay home. We were all disappointed because we were looking forward to attending. This weekend and today we have had several extended family members visit. This has been a blessing to have extra time with each.

Caring Bridge Log—Monday, June 20, 2011

We had a good weekend. Michael continues to be blessed by such thoughtful people! Thanks to each of you who have written notes, sent cards, or made special arrangements for him. You have so encouraged his heart!!!

For Father's Day, Grandpa came for dinner with Aunt Vicky and Uncle Rodger and my Chinese friend. We had a fun time together and played games. Michael's mind is sharp. We are thankful he still does not have any pain and has not had any more seizures. He has become somewhat weaker physically but is as independent as ever!

Michael picked out a fishing rod and reel for his dad for Father's Day. We hope to put it to use sometime this week. He loves to fish and usually catches more than his dad—mainly because Paul is busy taking them off the hook!

Thanks again for all your prayers and encouragement. I know I say this every time, but I truly mean it. We know this is what keeps us going and we continue to feel carried along by His grace. Please continue to pray for Paul and me, that we will have His wisdom and guidance in decisions that we make, and that His will will be done.

Journal—Wednesday, June 22, 2011

Things are better between Paul and I, less tension. I think we are both accepting what will happen—not trying to fix. Michael is weaker, down to 80 pounds. Great difficulty walking and balancing. Last weekend Paul and I picked out cemetery plots. The Lord has impressed on my heart to leave all to Him. Trust Him and know that He will do above and beyond all that we ask or think. Later in evening I read about Lazarus, Mary, and Martha. Mary's response to Lazarus's death and silence from Jesus—she prayed and stayed out of the way until called (John 11). Trust expecting God to answer, trust His heart. My new motto: Pray and stay out of the way!

Insight Now

Looking back at this time, there were so many decisions to make. We did not know when Michael would pass from this life, but we also did not want to be unprepared and scrambling at the last minute to make arrangements for his funeral and burial. We prayed about these decisions. A cemetery located a few miles from our home came to mind. We had been there when a friend of Paul's was laid to rest there. A beautiful old place by a country church. We purchased three plots for our family. A peaceful place, and peace in my heart.

Caring Bridge Log—Friday, June 24, 2011

Yesterday was a rough day for Michael. There are so many changes taking place physically and emotionally for him. He is not in pain and still no seizures, but he is living with reality. Thank you for praying for him and for us. Paul and I have God's peace through this—we are OK, just concerned for what Michael is going through.

Flashback

We were told Michael would have personality changes as a result of the brain tumor. There were times through his illness when he would become very angry, irrational, and at times would try to be physically aggressive (I learned to duck quickly!). A sword pierced my heart many times during those long months. This was not our sweet spirited boy. We would pray. We tried some different medication and dosages to treat these symptoms, but honestly they exacerbated his anxiety. So another medication was needed for the anxiety, which made him sleep most of the time. Then he would ask us to not give him medication because it made him feel weird. The main thing we wanted for him was peace. The decisions we made for Michael were difficult at times. We prayed about the different decisions each step of the way.

Insight Now

What gives me peace in all of this as I look back, is the fact that we cared for him at home, where we felt he could get the best care. And he wanted to be at home. Paul being able to be on family leave enabled this. (Thanks to his wonderful boss and supervisors! What a priceless gift!) Otherwise, I could not have cared for Michael by myself. We also tried to honor Michael's requests.

When my heart was hurting, I would cry it out to the Lord, and many times to my dear friend, Kim. When I am hurting, I want to be with someone who has the gift of mercy! Those who have walked through their own deep waters are so able to comfort others if they have yielded their hurt to God and not become bitter. Kim has eight babies in Heaven. No wonder she was able to show such mercy and compassion. She listened, prayed, and sympathized with me.

Journal—Wednesday, June 29, 2011

Doctor told us yesterday Michael may only have one or two months at most. This morning, praying about his funeral, God will do above and beyond all that we ask or think.

Caring Bridge Log—Thursday, June 30, 2011

This week we talked to the doctor about Michael's symptoms. He still is not in any pain and still no seizures for which we are thankful—but it is becoming increasingly difficult for him to walk and he has lost about fifteen pounds. (That's a lot for him.) His speech is slower also. She said his symptoms will probably snowball as time goes on and that he has only about a month or two to live. We told Michael in the beginning that we would not keep things from him and he wanted to hear what the doctor said. He handled it well.

Tomorrow I will be going to pick out a wheelchair for him.

Yesterday, we were encouraged by words from Hannah Whitall Smith:

> You have trusted Him in a few things, and He has not failed you. Trust Him now for everything, and see if He does not do for you exceeding abundantly above all that you could ever have asked or thought, not according to your power or capacity, but according to His own mighty power, that will work in you all the good pleasure of His most blessed will. You find no difficulty in trusting the Lord with the management of the universe and all the outward creation, and can your case be any more complex or difficult than these, that you need to be anxious or troubled about His management of it?[13]

So, we are trusting Him and we know, "His tender mercies are over all His works" (Psalm 145:9). And, I have heard that song Blessings by Laura Story. When I hear it I pray for all families who have loved ones struggling with cancer that we would all be drawn closer to the One who truly loves us and gave His life for us.

Tomorrow my friend is going to help me post some pictures of Michael fishing, and of his balloon ride that he had this week. What a fun time he had!

Insight Now

People using their gifts or what they have to bless us is such a gift of His love. My Uncle Ralph and Aunt Katie invited us often to a pond to fish. She even brought homemade pizza down one night for us to eat. And Uncle Ralph usually cleaned the fish! Michael loved fishing. When he could no longer hold the fishing pole, I would fish for him and he would just sit and watch. He loved it when I caught a big bass-- the biggest fish I had ever caught! The next time, Paul caught a big one too. We took pictures. His smile was hardly visible, and his eyes were not focused as before. But we knew there was joy in his heart, those were precious times.

The song "Blessings" by Laura Story is such a gift! I am so thankful that she allowed God to birth that song in her heart. My sister-in-law played it for me the first time I heard it, and I couldn't finish listening to it. The song was so timely for us as a family.

Journal—Sunday, July 3, 2011

Paul sick—we stayed home instead of going to church, and listened to a teaching and had communion. The Lord continues to impress on me to watch and wait and pray trustingly. Received a note from a friend telling us we are not alone in this. What comforting words! Later heard her husband on the radio talking about trials and difficulties in life. Was encouraged. The mower broke. Now we need a car and a mower. [One of our vehicles was no longer working.] Lord, you know our needs.

Caring Bridge Log—Tuesday, July 5, 2011

We had a quiet weekend. Michael and I both caught Paul's cold. Hopefully a milder version! Michael has been resting a lot and eating fried fish thanks to Uncle Ralph and Aunt Katie!

We listened to a teaching on the radio today about Heaven and keeping our focus on what is eternal. It was a good reminder.

Journal—Wednesday, July 6, 2011

Dan will fix the mower and Dave came to mow. [Paul's two brothers.]

Insight Now

What would we have done without these two guys? Such servant hearts! How blessed we were by their willingness to help when needed, frequently just from observing something that needed to be done— like Dave trimming Michael's nails numerous times during Michael's illness. Or reading to him. Eventually, when Michael was bedridden, it was almost a daily occurrence for Dave and Dan to come and watch old westerns on television with Michael, giving Paul and me a break. These things were such gifts to us!

Also, around this time, Uncle Ralph gave us a vehicle. What a huge blessing! Nicer than anything we have ever owned. God's servants, listening to God's heart, provide the most amazing blessings! Michael enjoyed riding in it to church and on fishing trips.

Yea, though I walk through the valley of the shadow of death,

I will fear no evil;

For You are with me;

Your rod and Your staff, they comfort me.

PSALM 23:4

CHAPTER FOUR

The Descent into the Valley

Journal—Saturday, July 16, 2011

God is so good. Continually feel impressed that He is working behind the scenes, even though I don't see it. Met with a friend this week. [Her son passed a few years ago from cancer.] Very encouraging and compassionate.

Flashback

This friend and I met in the 1970s when I lived in a Christian commune. We were reminiscing about what the Lord had done in our lives. I told her I remember sitting on the floor during a group prayer meeting in Eternity House and weeping. I think we were having communion. The Lord kept questioning me in my heart, "If I have to hurt you to use you, will you let Me?" In other words, will you unconditionally yield your life to me, no matter how painful it may become? Just the question had brought fear and pain to my heart. And yet I felt such love for Him, in light of all that He had done for me. How could I say no? But I hesitated to say yes. And each time I hesitated, He would ask again. Eventually, I told Him yes.

Elisabeth Elliot says about pain, "Like a skilled surgeon, God may have to hurt us, but He will never harm us."[14]

Caring Bridge Log—Tuesday, July 19, 2011

Thank you to all of you for your prayers, encouragement, support, offers to help and acts of kindness! Each of you has blessed us and we are in awe of such kindness!

Michael does not want to go anywhere but church now. He is not able to stand on his own. Paul carried him (piggyback) into church last Sunday, rather than Michael trying to walk. Paul is so, so good with him! Michael does not want to use the wheelchair at this time, even though we have one. He continues to deteriorate. He is getting harder to understand when he talks and is eating less, though I am trying to cook his favorites. He has the same sweet spirit and tender heart. He still does not have any pain and there have not been any more seizures.

The Lord gives us such courage and strength through this. Today when I was thinking about what may lie ahead, the Lord reassured me. II Corinthians 3:18 came to mind, "But we all, with unveiled face, beholding as in a mirror the glory of the Lord, are being transformed into the same image from glory to glory, just as by the Spirit of the Lord." As we focus on Him in these difficult times we are transformed from one stage of glory to another. And the words He spoke to my heart, "Don't be afraid of what is ahead!" were such a comfort. God is so faithful! He truly is there when I need Him!!!

Journal—Wednesday, July 20, 2011

All that has previously taken place, God has used to mold me and prepare me for where I am at on this journey; many of the things that I did not want but endured. They are what God has used to fashion me thus far. (Like a potter, fashioning a lump of clay into something useful.) What I face in the future He will use to fashion me more. His words to me, "Don't be afraid of what lies ahead! Don't be afraid of life without Michael." God will be there. Live selflessly. God will work in others. Trust Him more.

Caring Bridge Log—Thursday, July 28, 2011

We continue to be blessed by cards, notes, prayers and help from so many caring people. Thank you so much!!! These things make such a difference in our lives. I can't imagine walking this path without God and the support from others.

Michael had a difficult day yesterday. Little things are much more challenging and frustrating to him. Physically and emotionally he continues to deteriorate. Please pray that God will carry him through this and that His will would be done.

Journal—Thursday, July 28, 2011

Last night, Michael and Paul were praying together. Paul prayed, "God, if it be Your will, please take me instead of Michael." Later, Michael told me what God impressed on him—Paul not ready. Then I asked if God indicated anything about me—not ready. And what about himself? Michael started crying and said God told him He was going to take him. Sobbing. So hard for him to accept. I just prayed that God would give him peace and comfort. While jogging this morning, God impressed on my heart He would send comfort.

Caring Bridge Log—Saturday, July 30, 2011

Please pray for Michael today. He is starting to have a difficult day. It is hard for him to accept everything. Thank you very much for all your prayers. They are greatly appreciated.

Journal—Monday, August 1, 2011

Still difficult for Michael to accept. Major frustrations over things. Saying things I know he does not mean, things totally out of character. Canceled some scheduled visits with others because of his behavior. Only want to visit with family from now on. Later he apologizes, but he gets so worked up!

Flashback

Michael's behavior changes were unpredictable. I don't know how much was the tumor and how much the medication. At times it was heartbreaking. I would just keep crying out to God to help us, to give us wisdom and give Michael peace. But we also set some boundaries about who came to visit. We did not want others to experience Michael's behavior changes, it was difficult enough for family.

Journal—Monday, August 8, 2011

Woke up at 2:45a.m. and still awake. Two nights ago I dreamed that my friend from high school and I were running in a very long distance race over very rocky ground—steep in places. I was wondering if I could make it and then I heard the voice of one of God's undershepherds calling from afar, "Go Joni, keep going!" Encouraging me to persevere, to not stop. Then I woke up.

Flashback

Around this time, I ran into an acquaintance whose husband had died of cancer. We talked about the challenges of caring for someone who is dying. She told me that there would be time to grieve later.

"Right now, she said, "it is like you are leading a parade and many people are following you and depending on you. You can't stop. If you stop, it affects everyone who is behind you. So, you just keep going and later there will be time to grieve."

This resonated loudly in my heart. I felt so validated and encouraged by her words because that was exactly how my life was being lived out—the cooking, dishes, laundry, cleaning, grocery shopping, and details that a wife and mom take care of. Although, I confess, I had great friends and relatives who came to help me often. What a gift they were! But, I always had to keep going. There was no time to stop and regroup, no time to process all the changes in our lives. I couldn't take a day away. I did get up each morning and read the Bible and try to jog. That was my prayer time—invaluable in pouring out my heart to the Lord.

Every morning when I was just waking up, my first thoughts would be of Michael and what he was going through—the jarring reality; it was not a bad dream, it was real life. This started when we first saw the MRI and continued until he passed from this life.

Caring Bridge Log—Friday, August 12, 2011

Thank you for your continued prayers. The last week has had its ups and downs, but God continues to give us the grace and strength we need. Michael continues to deteriorate, thankfully without pain and without any seizures. We took him fishing this week, it was finally cool enough! He cannot cast or reel in his line. Paul fished for him. Paul's line caught several bullheads that he threw back. Michael caught a large painted turtle! It was a beautiful afternoon and he enjoyed being outside. And they had enough for me to fry for dinner.

In our Bible readings this week several things came up and we share them with you because they have been a help to us in going through difficulties. Maybe this will help to understand how we view healing and God's sovereignty. A commentary on Philippians 2 about healing says,

> Ultimately, everyone will be healed, for by Jesus' stripes, we are all healed (Isaiah 53:5). The only question is timing. When they ask for healing, some are healed immediately; others, five years later; others, not until they get to heaven. Healing has nothing to do with a person's spirituality or faith. It has everything to do with God's sovereignty.

> Three times Paul prayed for deliverance, only to hear the Lord say, "No, Paul. When you are weak, then My strength is manifested. My grace is sufficient for you" (2 Corinthians 12:9). Thus, I encourage those who are afflicted to follow Paul's model, to pray three times, thirty times, or three hundred times--until they receive what they're asking for, or until they have a peace in their heart that says, "This is what the Lord has for me, and I can embrace it." [15]

Then yesterday, I was reading Job 13:15, where Job says, "Though He slay me, yet will I trust Him." A commentary says,

"Even if I don't understand what God is doing, even though it seems to me to be unfair, even if He should slay me in the process, yet I will trust Him," Job proclaims. . .

It's one thing to have faith for healing. It's a greater thing to have faith for sickness. That is, it takes greater faith to say, "I come to You for healing. But, Lord, should You, as You did to Paul, say, 'My grace is sufficient,' I will still trust You. I have faith in You, not faith that I can get You to do what I want You to do, but faith that You will do what's best."

Even if the affliction doesn't go away, even if the problem continues, even if the solution doesn't come, faith says, "Though You slay me, I will still trust You because You were slain for me. You gave up everything because You love me. Therefore, I embrace whatever You decide to do. You see things I don't. You know things I don't. You know things I can't."

Here, with his body broken out in boils, with his worldly possessions and his family taken from him, with his friends relentlessly accusing him, faith flares up in Job. [16]

We continue to pray daily for Michael's healing and for all of God's will to be done on earth as it is in Heaven. But we also trust Him to do what is best this side of Heaven. Knowing His great love for us gives us a peace in our hearts.

Journal—Monday, August 15, 2011

Sunday morning very difficult. Michael flip-flopped numerous times about going to church. Wailing. So hard to watch. [He said he wanted to go and we would start getting him ready, and then he would say he didn't want to go. So, we would decide to stay home and he would become upset and want to go ... round and round.] We went a half hour late but decided not to do this again. Too hard on him. He said on the way there, "I feel weak."

Journal—Wednesday, August 17, 2011

Monday night Michael was in pain in his hip joint. We wonder if he had a seizure. Crying, scared, breathing off. Paul and I both thought he might be dying. Michael later said in his mind he saw something evil. We told him to tell us when he senses evil and we will pray. Paul then read him the story of Elisha. Elisha's servant is afraid because they are surrounded by their enemies. Elisha tells him,

"'Do not fear, for those who are with us are more than those who are with them.' And Elisha prayed, and said, 'Lord, I pray, open his eyes that he may see.' Then the Lord opened the eyes of the young man, and he saw. And behold, the mountain was full of horses and chariots of fire all around Elisha" (II Kings 6:16-17).

Caring Bridge Log—Thursday, August 18, 2011

We just posted a picture of Michael's latest fishing excursion. I caught a big fish on Michael's pole—a miraculous answer to prayer! Fishing is one of the few things he still enjoys. (Even if mom and dad have to hold the pole for him). Being outside enjoying God's creation is very refreshing for all of us.

Michael continues to have days when he's happy and content and days when it is a struggle. Thanks to all of you for your prayers, cards and support. I know I say this over and over again, but these things make such a difference in our lives and we are truly grateful.

Journal—Monday August 22, 2011

This morning jogging it was cloudy at sunrise. The sun shone through the narrow band between the horizon and the clouds. Then went completely out of sight behind the clouds. Felt impressed that we are entering a dark time and will feel like the sun is gone. Trust that it is still shining.

Caring Bridge Log—Friday, August 26, 2011

Just posted a picture of Paul's latest fishing catch. The competition continues! And yes, Michael has enjoyed eating fried fish!

Journal Saturday, August 27, 2011

Last night Michael upset over stomach pains. Gave him something for this. It helped but he was crying "Why do I have to suffer?" He prayed that God would take him. Today he brought up the subject of his funeral. Said he hoped his favorite Bible teacher would be able to speak at it. Something to pray about.

Insight Now

Why did Michael have to suffer? Why did Paul and I have to watch, feeling helpless at times? All I could do was cry out to God. And that was enough, because I know He hears, He sees, He cares. Isaiah 63:9 is a comfort:

"In all their affliction He was afflicted, and the Angel of His Presence saved them; in His love and in His pity He redeemed them; and He bore them and carried them all the days of old."

And if He allows suffering in this world, He will work it for good in the lives of His children. II Corinthians 4:16-18 says:

> Therefore we do not lose heart. Even though our outward man is perishing, yet the inward man is being renewed day by day. For our light affliction, which is but for a moment, is working for us a far more exceeding and eternal weight of glory, while we do not look at the things which are seen, but at the things which are not seen. For the things which are seen are temporary, but the things which are not seen are eternal.

Can I endure, knowing that He is working things for greater glory than I can imagine—eternally, not just presently? Yes, by His grace! Even now, as I write this book, it is at times so painful, reliving certain moments—and missing Michael terribly! But God's grace is here.

Michael didn't really want to talk much about his funeral, other than that he wanted his message played and whom he wanted to officiate. I prayed much about this. We had been to funerals, but had not planned one. Paul's parents had passed before we were married, as well as most of our grandparents—just my mom's mother was still living. I don't remember exactly when, but around this time, I was on my knees praying and asking God to orchestrate Michael's funeral, the order of things, the music, the speakers. God just brought the thoughts to my mind and helped me with the details. Paul approved of it all. Once again, God showed us His faithfulness by helping us.

Caring Bridge Log—Thursday, September 1, 2011

Thank you for your continued prayers. Michael has had a difficult week. He has become physically weaker and depends upon us for his complete care. He began using his wheelchair this week because he needs support while sitting. Today we ordered a hospital bed that will help him be more comfortable at home. His speech is harder to understand. He still has such a sweet spirit though and last night thanked me. He keeps wanting me to sing to him at night, so I sing songs about peace.

Flashback

Initially, Michael was very resistive in using the wheelchair and later the hospital bed. I think he saw them as a sign of weakness. But, they were both very helpful. The wheelchair was necessary because he needed support while sitting and could no longer walk; carrying him was difficult. The hospital bed made it easier for him when we wanted give him something to eat or drink while he was in bed. It also had rails so he could not fall out. Eventually he accepted them.

Journal—Thursday, September 1, 2011

Will he make it through this month? He has become very weak. Last night, I said to him, "I'm sorry I haven't been a better mom." He put his hand on my arm (which is difficult at this point for him to do—he has quit waving at people). Then he told me I was a good mom. He thanked me for homeschooling him and for making science fun.

These days have seemed long.

Insight Now

Spurgeon says about this:

> Cheerfulness is the support of our strength; in the joy of
> the Lord are we strong. It acts as the remover of difficulties.
> It is to our service what oil is to the wheels of a railway car-
> riage. Without oil the axle soon grows hot, and accidents
> occur; and if there be not a holy cheerfulness to oil our
> wheels, our spirits will be clogged with weariness.[17]

How I need to give thanks to God, and praise and worship Him,
especially during days that seem long! It changes my perspective and
my attitude. Lord, help me serve You with gladness!

Caring Bridge Log—Thursday, September 8, 2011

Thank you for your continued prayers. Michael still does not have
any pain and we are very thankful for this answer to prayer. In the
last two days, his speech is less discernible and he continues to grow
weaker. He still has difficult days but we are trying to encourage him
and comfort him.

I have been reading to him from the children's version of Hinds'
Feet on High Places. We had read it years ago but it is a very timely
book to read about Much-Afraid's journey to the high places to be
with the Good Shepherd. The two companions He has given her are
Sorrow and Suffering. As she accepts her two companions and the path
the Shepherd has for her, she grows in strength and trust and is transformed on this journey. The author, Hannah Hurnard, writes:

> Finally after such a long time, the path that Much-Afraid and

her two helpers traveled had turned toward the High Places! Much-Afraid fell on her knees and worshiped. It seemed to her at that moment that all the pain and all the troubles had been worthwhile.[18]

This book has opened the door to some good conversations about suffering and accepting the path that God has for each of us.

Journal—Wednesday, September 5, 2011

Have been reading to Michael out of *Hinds' Feet on High Places*. Michael said the characters, Sorrow and Suffering, are really Dumb and Stupid.[19] [We normally don't condone name calling!] He has been listening and tearful at times during the reading though. Surrendering our own will, acceptance with joy, and trusting the Good Shepherd are all very relevant topics right now.

Tonight it was painful for him getting ready for bed. Called Paul and I "the tormentors." He said I was Bloody Mary and Paul was Henry VIII. What a riot!

Insight Now

It was so hard not to laugh at Michael's statement, partly because it was so out of character for him to say such a thing! I don't mean to seem heartless. The irony of these two parents trying to lovingly care for their son 24/7, and then being compared to those two individuals! My homeschooling mentor later said, "Well, he certainly knows his history!" We had studied them the year before.

Who knows why he said these things. Paul and I tried so hard to give him the best care possible in our home because we loved him so much. When he would get angry sometimes, we just came to accept that it was the cancer, the medication and probably just immense frustration of being a teenager and not being able to care for himself—especially when dad and mom were the caregivers. It was his choice for us to be his caregivers. He would allow the home healthcare nurse to only take his vital signs. One minute he would be his sweet self and the next, angry with one or both of us. We tried to love and honor him and treat him like we would want to be treated.

Journal—Tuesday, September 13, 2011

My thirty-fifth high school class reunion is this Friday and Saturday. My friend is coming from Colorado. We keep wondering if Michael is going to make it much longer. God continues to impress on my heart to trust Him with all things and let Him work. Pray and stay out of the way. Isaiah 55:8–9, "'For My thoughts are not your thoughts, nor are your ways My ways,' says the Lord. 'For as the heavens are higher than the earth, so are My ways higher than your ways, and My thoughts than your thoughts.'"

Caring Bridge Log—Wednesday, September 14, 2011

Just a quick update. Michael told us this morning that he is having some pain in his hands and hips, but he does not want any pain medication. I think it is worse when he has been moved. He is sleeping more during the day and sleeps well at night. We are thankful that he still does not have any headaches. We finished *Hinds Feet on High Places* and I asked him what he would like me to read next. He answered, "Read it again." So, we are!

Journal—Friday, September 16, 2011

Tonight was the class reunion. Last night Michael said he didn't want me to go. So I didn't tonight, but will tomorrow night (the location will be closer, ten minutes from our house).

Journal—Saturday, September 17, 2011

At Saturday night reunion, talked to so many. Great talks, tearful talks. So glad I went. Gave out the address of Michael's Caring Bridge site to many.

Insight Now

Friends are such a blessing! Friend from Colorado had brought numerous gifts for Michael—rocks, fossils, sharks' teeth—all things he loves and is interested in. She was always buying him too much! And then she and another friend had come for lunch. The other friend had made Michael a pillowcase that a fisherman would love. The material had pictures of fish and fishing tackle all over it. It was special and he liked it. Very thoughtful of them both.

Caring Bridge Log—Sunday, September 18, 2011

What a blessing it was to attend my class reunion last night and receive so many words of encouragement and hugs! Thanks to all my classmates who are watching Michael's Caring Bridge site and praying for him. We are so grateful for everyone's support during this time.

Michael is still having some pain in his hips when we move him, but his hands have not been hurting anymore.

Journal—Wednesday, September 21, 2011

Read in *Joy and Strength* a poem by A. H. Francke:

> In Thy might all things I bear,
> In Thy love find bitter sweet,
> And with all my grief and care,
> Sit in patience at Thy feet.[20]

Caring Bridge Log—Friday, September 23, 2011

Michael has grown weaker and is eating very little. He can not drink regular liquids so we feed him watermelon or ice cream. His hands and feet are frequently cold. He also has a low grade fever. He spends most of his time in the hospital bed. All of these are normal symptoms for the final stages of brain cancer. We are so thankful to have him at home with us and to have a home health care nurse visit us weekly.

He talks very little and is hard to understand but he still has his sense of humor and has pain only briefly when we move him.

Journal—Friday, September 23, 2011

Paul said to Michael tonight, "What I miss most is your smile." [He is no longer able to smile.]

Michael said, "When you get to Heaven, I'll be the first one to greet you with it!"

He is so sweet!

Last night, while Paul outside, Michael asked tearfully, "Why don't I have peace?" I told him that sometimes God withdraws our sense of His presence to stretch our faith and see if we really trust Him instead of our feelings. So, we prayed and he told God he trusted Him.

Later that evening, when watching a movie, Michael looked at us and said, "Am I in Heaven?"

We said, "No, why?"

He told us he felt a warm peace and it felt so good he thought he was in Heaven. I told him I thought God gave him a glimpse of what was to come and that it was the tip of the iceberg!

Insight Now

God is so faithful! Yes, His Word promises us peace that passes understanding. But, honestly, there are times when I don't feel it or I just feel numb. It does not mean though, that God does not see, or does not hear, or does not care. He does. Sometimes, He just wants me to trust Him and set my feelings aside. I am so glad Michael got this lesson and that God rewarded him with this glimpse of what Heaven will be like.

Streams in the Desert for September 22 gives a quote from Charles H. Spurgeon addressing this issue:

> Our faith is the center of the target God aims at when he tests us... There is nothing that pierces faith to its very marrow—to find whether or not it is the faith of those who are immortal—like shooting the arrow of the feeling of being deserted into it. And only genuine faith will escape unharmed from the midst of the battle after having been stripped of its armor of earthly enjoyment and after having endured the circumstances coming against it that the powerful hand of God has allowed.

Faith must be tested, and the sense of feeling deserted is "the furnace heated seven times hotter than usual" (Dan. 3:19) into which it may be thrown. Blessed is the person who endures such an ordeal! [21]

Journal—Monday, September 26, 2011

Michael in bed most of yesterday and today. At homeschool soccer they had a bake sale for us. What a blessing!

Last night, Michael asked me why he got cancer. I told him I did not know why, or what caused it, but I did tell him what God told me last March after the MRI, (that He was taking Michael because He delighted in him). Michael cried. I did not know that earlier in the evening, Paul had told him that God delighted in him and here I was telling him the same statement. What timing!

Journal—Wednesday, September 28, 2011

Michael wants someone with him all the time. He wanted *Hind's Feet on High Places* read to him today. We were at the part about putting everything on the altar. [22] A kind family gave us a movie that was made of this book. When it came to the place where Much-Afraid was going to meet the Good Shepherd, he sobbed, "I want to go be with the Shepherd!" He was also tearful this morning, missing people in Oregon. But did not want to try to talk with them, probably because he can't speak clearly.

Caring Bridge Log—Wednesday, September 28, 2011

Michael has asked us to post a prayer request. He would like us to pray for God's timing. Last night he told us he wanted to go be with the Good Shepherd.

He is very weak and has had very little fluids today. He is still able to talk with us although it is hard to understand him. We are so thankful that he does not have any pain.

Today we were reading in Isaiah 45, verse 9. A commentary was helpful at this time. It says:

> In itself, clay is relatively worthless. But in the hands of the potter with a picture in his mind of what he wants to create, it can become something of beauty. Do you ever feel like you're going in circles, that you're being pushed and poked and prodded? If you do, consider yourself blessed because it means the Master Potter is transforming you into a vessel He can use. The Lord knows what He's doing, so don't fight against it because if you fight against God and "win," you lose. If you demand your way and God finally says, "Okay, have your way," you're in trouble. Most of the time, people fight against God because they mistakenly think He is going to do less than the best for them. If we really believed that God only wants to do things that are exceedingly abundantly above all we can ask or think, that His plan for us is to make the worthless clay of our lives into something beautiful and useful, we wouldn't fight against Him. [23]

So, please pray for God's will and timing in Michael going home and in all the plans to follow. Thank you for your prayers. We are so blessed to be surrounded by such caring people!

Journal—Monday, October 3, 2011

Michael up at 4:00 a.m. Last few days have felt I am on the verge of a vast dry, desolate desert. It is hard not to dread it or be afraid. But the best thing I can do is honor the Lord by trusting and yielding to Him whatever He wants to do.

Michael has mellowed out—not so angry and agitated. He is so sweet. How our lives are going to change without him.

Caring Bridge Log—Wednesday, October 5, 2011

Today I read in *Joy and Strength* a quote by A. C. A. Hall: "Thanksgiving for the past makes us trustful in the present and hopeful for the future."[24]

Jesus is so faithful to us and we love Him so much, He gives us such peace.

Please continue to pray for God's timing and for all the details to be orchestrated according to God's will.

Caring Bridge Log—Monday, October 10, 2011

We had a quiet weekend. Michael stays in bed all the time now. And eats little. We don't know how much time he has left on this side of Heaven. Some days he seems so weak and other days he seems stronger. He still does not have any pain for which we are thankful.

Read recently in *Finding Your Way Through Loneliness*, a book by Elisabeth Elliot, a quote after her first husband was killed,

> I say that I found peace. I do not say that I was not lonely,
> I was—terribly. I do not say that I did not grieve. I did—
> most sorely. But peace of the sort the world cannot give

comes, not by the removal of suffering, but in another way—through acceptance.[25]

Although her loss was sudden and ours is gradual, God's peace is there as we continually surrender ourselves to Him who gave everything for us.

Journal—Wednesday, October 12, 2011

Michael said today that God told him that He was going to take him soon. He seems a little sad about this.

Read in *Finding Your Way Through Loneliness* by Elisabeth Elliot, about a girl who "had no agenda of her own" and how:

"The heart which has no agenda but God's is the heart at leisure from itself. Its emptiness is filled with the Love of God. Its solitude can be turned into prayer."[26]

Have read and heard a lot lately on being willing to do whatever He calls me to do. Be available.

Journal—Monday, October 24, 2011

Long days these have been—some of the hardest for me and I feel weary. Feel suspended. On Saturday, Michael and I were listening to the radio and heard a song that was played when we were at morning worship in Oregon. We both began to cry. So sad. I just prayed.

Caring Bridge Log—Monday, October 24, 2011

Thank you for your prayers, comments, cards and letters—we are so blessed by the outpouring of love in so many different ways! Michael seems to have plateaued. We are amazed and so is his doctor. Still no pain for which we are so very thankful! Honestly, the days have seemed long as of late, but Paul and I both are glad that Michael is able to be at home with us and not in the hospital. I've been making pumpkin and apple pies for him—his favorites. He has not lost his sense of humor and is finding new ways to play tricks on us even though he is confined to his hospital bed!

A few days ago we received a copy of this in the mail. It was so timely and helpful. It is from *Come Away My Beloved* by Frances J. Roberts:

> Behold, My hand is upon you to bless you and to accomplish all My good purpose. For this hour I have prepared your heart; and in My kindness I will not let you fail.
>
> Only relinquish all things into My hands; for I can work freely only as you release Me by complete committal—both of yourself and others. As was written of old: "Commit your way to the LORD; trust also in Him; and He shall bring it to pass" (Psa. 37:5). I will be your sustaining strength; and My peace shall garrison your mind. Only TRUST ME—all I do is done in love.
>
> Adversities are a necessity. They are part of the pattern of life's pilgrimage for every individual; and who can escape them? But I say to you, that for those who walk in Me, and for those who are encircled by the intercessory prayers of My children, I will make of the suffering, yes, I shall make of the trials a stepping-stone to future blessing ... My arms are around you, and never have I loved you more! [27]

This blessed me because so much is uncertain for us now and in the future. But we can trust Him even in the fog of uncertainty.

Journal—Tuesday, October 26, 2011

Read in a commentary on Jeremiah 34 about not holding others captive because of past sins, forgiving them. Should release them and resist temptation to bind them again. [28]

Insight Now

Wounded people wound people. During Michael's illness, sometimes the responses of people would hurt terribly, usually the closer the tie, the deeper the wound. Why is it so much easier to forgive a total stranger? And I am sure I have hurt others terribly. The Lord just kept impressing on my heart to love, to not take up an offense and to see myself as a sinner also in need of the Lord's forgiveness. This sounds very easy, but at times it is one of the hardest things for me, especially when my pride has been hurt. But, it is also God's way of humbling me and teaching me again to forgive as He has forgiven me. It is a choice, not a feeling. There are times when I have had to set boundaries or speak the truth in love—but my main response needs to be to extend grace, because grace has been extended to me. "Hatred stirs up strife, but love covers all sins" (Proverbs 10:12). Then I can be free of resentment. My mind can be at peace, thinking on what is truly good.

Journal—Monday, October 31, 2011

Hard weekend. Wishing for someone to come and make it all better. Read today in Elisabeth Elliot's book, *Finding Your Way Through Loneliness*:

Suffering is a wilderness experience. We feel very much alone and helpless, cut off from others who cannot know how we suffer. We long for someone to come to our aid, be "company" for us, get us out of this. Someone will. Some One will certainly come to our aid. He will be company for us if we'll let Him. But get us out of it? Not necessarily.[29]

Caring Bridge Log—Wednesday, November 2, 2011

Yesterday was such a beautiful day here. We are glad that Michael has his hospital bed by the window so he can look out and see the fall colors! Michael continues to be pain free and still eating pie.

We read a quote from Elisabeth Elliot's book, *Finding Your Way through Loneliness*, which was very timely. She was talking to a woman who was diagnosed with a sudden illness that would leave her incapacitated. The woman had asked her what good she would be to God if she were bedridden. Elisabeth Elliot replied:

> So we had to talk about God's idea of "good"—very different from mere utilitarianism. He wanted her to trust and obey.... The only way she could learn trust and obedience was to have things happen which she could not understand. That is where faith begins—in the wilderness, when you are alone and afraid, when things don't make sense. She must hang on to the message of the Cross: God loves you. He loved you enough to die for you. Will you trust Him?...A pure faith would be worth far more to God than all the service she had hoped to render if poor

health had not interrupted her plans. [30]

Reading this has helped me to once again remember that His perspective is so different from mine—but I can trust Him! Thank you again for all your prayers! We are truly blessed!

Caring Bridge Log—Tuesday, November 8, 2011

On Wednesday, November 9th, we would like to have a day of prayer for Michael. He wants to go be with his Good Shepherd, but also wants God's timing—not his own. Please pray for him to have courage and patience in waiting on the Lord. And please pray for Paul and me to have God's wisdom and guidance in all the decisions we make. Thank you for all your prayers.

Journal—Wednesday, November 9, 2011

Day of prayer for Michael. Not understanding the delay, but trusting Him. Last Sunday night, Michael in a rage, worst we have seen. We do not understand.

Insight Now

Michael was usually an easy going, cheerful kid. He had a sweetness about him, a kindness. How many times had I told him, "What is desired in a man is kindness" (Proverbs 19:22)?

So, when he would get so angry, it seemed totally out of character. Recently, I have heard of others who suffered from brain cancer and how similar aggression would happen. We were warned of this also. But at the time, it was one of the hardest things to watch. I was afraid that these memories of him so angry would overshadow all the good memories. Now, I realize that they overshadowed them only for a time, like a passing dark cloud.

Journal—*Thursday, November 10, 2011*

Michael seems weaker. Was swinging his fist at me this morning. Raging when I tried to lift his head to wipe off his hair. Then slept the rest of the morning.

Journal—*Friday, November 11, 2011*

Read from Fenelon:

> Don't be so concerned about the future. The future belongs to God. He is in charge of all things and will take care of you completely. If you try to guess what is going to happen you will only worry yourself and anticipate trouble. Live each day as it comes. Each day brings it own good and evil, but what seems evil becomes good if you leave it in God's hands. Do not hold up His purpose by being impatient.
>
> God has a time for everything. Never second guess Him. One of the most important things you must do is live in the present moment. It is not how fast you go, but how well you go. God knows just how long it will take you to get from one place to another. You needn't always be rushing about. Simply follow God's leading.
>
> All you need to do is prepare your heart by giving it completely over to God, without reservation. He will do with you what He pleases. Close your eyes and follow Him. Walk, as Abraham did, not knowing where you are going.

God Himself will be your guide. He will lead you through the desert to the Promised Land. You will be so happy if you let God take full control of your life! [31]

Stay in the present, trust God and surrender all to Him. Don't guess what will happen. Yield to Him completely.

Caring Bridge Log—Friday, November 11, 2011

Thanks so much to each of you for all your prayers and encouragement, especially on Michael's day of prayer. Michael told me to thank you, too! Outwardly I can't see any changes, but I know the Lord is at work.

Today we read from *Morning and Evening*, based on Psalm 47:4 (KJV) "He shall choose our inheritance for us." He writes:

> Believer, if your inheritance be a lowly one you should be satisfied with your earthly portion; for you may rest assured that it is the fittest for you. Unerring wisdom ordained your lot, and selected for you the safest and best condition. A ship of large tonnage is to be brought up the river; now, in one part the stream there is a sandbank; should some one ask, 'Why does the captain steer through the deep part of the channel and deviate so much from a straight line?' His answer would be, 'Because I should not get my vessel into harbour at all if I did not keep the deep channel'. So it may be, you would run aground and suffer shipwreck, if your divine Captain did not steer you into the depths of affliction where waves of trouble follow each other in quick succession. Some plants die if they have too much

sunshine. It may be that you are planted where you get but little, you are put there by the loving Husbandman, because only in that situation will you bring forth fruit unto perfection. Remember this, had any other condition been better for you than the one in which you are, divine love would have put you there. You are placed by God in the most suitable circumstances, and if you had the choosing of your lot, you would soon cry, 'Lord, choose my inheritance for me for by my self-will I am pierced through with many sorrows'. Be content with such things as you have, since the Lord has ordered all things for your good. Take up your own daily cross; it is the burden best suited for your shoulder, and will prove most effective to make you perfect in every good word and work to the glory of God. Down busy self, and proud impatience, it is not for you to choose, but for the Lord of Love! [32]

This speaks to me of so many things. As difficult as it is to daily watch Michael deteriorate, his spiritual faith has grown and this blesses Paul and me. Some have said to us they wonder at our strength in this. But I would tell you, it is truly the Lord—we are weak people. And this is what the Lord has for us and He gives us the grace we need when we need it. I look at the trials of others and think what we are enduring could be much more difficult. I believe the Lord sovereignly rules over the lives of each of His children and as we yield to Him, He makes all things bearable and works them for good and best of all is with us in the difficulties. So, what someone else endures amazes me, but I am not called to their path, I am to walk my own and trust that it has been hand picked by my loving Lord, Whose grace is sufficient for me.

Thank you again for all your prayers, and if the Lord uses any of what we are learning to bless you or encourage you on your journey, to Jesus be all the glory!!!

Journal—Monday, November 14, 2011

We backed off on his medication in October and he did better eating and drinking, but he had major meltdowns. So we are giving him some medicine every other day. More tired again and eating less. Feel impressed to get things ready. Lord, please work out all these details according to your will.

Journal—Thursday, November 17, 2011

Tonight Bethany Dorin dropped off a CD recording of "Michael's Song" that the Lord had given her. It is fabulous! I love it! God, please let someone record it for Your church that needs to hear this in the days ahead. Please use this song for Your glory.

These are the words:

Let your heart not be troubled nor let fears arise.
Peace He's promised His people, and so He will supply.

Peace I give to you. Not the world's but Mine.
Let your heart not be troubled. Trust in God and Him alone.

God is good and He's mighty, He is just and great.
Our Father and Guardian. Our Keeper and our Friend.

Chorus

As the world shakes at trouble and the earth at pain.
You stand firm on this promise and never ever wane.

Let God's peace that's surpassing give you strength to pray
To your God and your Maker Who's with you all the way. [33]

Caring Bridge Log—Tuesday, November 22, 2011

We are so thankful this Thanksgiving week for so many things—for all your prayers, for all your encouragement and kindness, for God's faithfulness. and for Christ's promise of peace to us! We hope each of you enjoy your Thanksgiving holiday.

Thank you for praying for Michael last night. His headache is gone. He does not seem to want food this morning and only a sip of tea so far. But he still wants mom to cook a turkey on Thursday!

Journal—Wednesday, November 23, 2011

Michael had a major meltdown tonight. So hard to watch. Hysterical. Don't know what to do or think. Is it spiritual? Is it the cancer? What and how do we deal with it? Why aren't my prayers enough?

Insight Now

Many, many times during the course of Michael's illness people had encouraged me to have this or that person or group pray for Michael's healing. We had simply obeyed scripture and taken him to be anointed with oil and prayed over by the pastor and elders. Michael himself got discouraged when other people would pray for him and there was not any change. So, I think that with people literally all over the world praying for Michael, God would have healed him this side of Heaven if it was His timing. And sometimes, He allows us to walk through the valley of the shadow of death. I don't ever want someone to feel that if they just had more "faith," God would have healed them. Blaming those who are hurting is not helpful. I want to pray and trust God to do what is best. Jesus' prayer in the Garden of Gethsemane was, "O My Father, if it is possible, let this cup pass from Me; nevertheless, not as I will, but as You will" (Matthew 26:39).

In the movie, *The Hiding Place*, Betsie told Corrie that the Lord had told her they would both be released by the New Year.[34] They were, but not in the way they thought. Betsie was ill and went to Heaven, and Corrie was set free from the prison camp. It was God's sovereign way of releasing each of them—His way, His perspective, not theirs.

Caring Bridge Log—Monday, November 28, 2011

We had a good Thanksgiving. Grandpa and Grandma came for dinner. Michael ate a few bites of turkey, dressing and mashed potatoes and gravy. Since then his appetite has decreased.

Last night about 12:30 am, Michael had a seizure. It lasted about an hour. At first we thought he was experiencing pain, but then we noticed some twitching and realized what was happening. We were able to give him medicine that helped, and since then have increased his seizure medication.

Today he is less able to speak and drink and is physically weaker. We are giving him fluids through a dropper. He hasn't wanted much to eat and is sleeping more than usual.

This isn't the time of the year I would have picked to go through this but God continues to impress on my heart to trust Him. It is a challenge for me to thank and praise Him in faith this side of Heaven not understanding how all of this is going to be worked for good. I want to have a heart of complete trust in Him though.

Journal—Friday, December 2, 2011

I can't believe we are still in this in December—but God must have his reasons. Michael is weaker, can hardly understand him. He is sweeter most of the time. He eats a few bites. Increase in medicine seems to help. Most of the day he is calm. If Michael passes this month it will be difficult, especially with several birthdays and Christmas. Lord, what are you doing? I feel so suspended and want this chapter of my life to be over. But Lord, Your will be done, not mine.

Insight Now

If I had known then that Michael would not pass from this life until the end of January, I would have despaired greatly. Thankfully, God usually does not reveal the future to us! It was so hard to watch the seizures. Also, at night Paul and I would take turns sleeping on a bed next to his hospital bed. Many, many long nights. We would get so tired from lack of sleep. And I would feel so torn in my heart. I didn't want to be parted from Michael, but I didn't want to see him suffer. I would feel guilty over feelings of wanting to be free of this suffering, for him, for Paul and for me. I would feel guilty over not giving him better care. And then, not knowing why the suffering continued. God had His reasons. The following helps:

> In Bible times, when a man wanted to make something
> of fine gold, he would subject the ore to such intense heat

that all of the impurities would be burned out. The gold-smith would know that the work was done when he could see the reflection of his own face in the liquefied gold.

The same thing is true with us. The Lord says, "I've got big plans for you, huge plans. I've got plans not for this life only, but for eternity. Therefore, I may need to turn up the heat a bit to work out the impurities. But My hand is on the thermostat. I know exactly what I'm doing. Although at the present moment, it might not be easy, you'll thank Me for the next billion years to come because what I'm after is to see the reflection of My face in your life."...What we really want is to be like Him. There are things in our lives that keep that from happening, so the way He deals with them is to turn up the heat a bit in order that we'll come out of the fire stronger in faith and more like the Lord.... When you finally understand this, you'll rejoice in difficulty rather than rebel because you'll see it as a purifying process that will work wonderful things into your life. Tribulation works patience. When you're going through difficulty, there's not a lot you can do other than wait for the master goldsmith to finish the process. Patience, in turn works experience as we learn that God truly knows what He's doing. Experience works hope—the absolute expectation of coming good. [35]

Caring Bridge Log—Sunday, December 4, 2011

Thank you for praying for Michael. His headache was gone when he woke up this morning.

This afternoon he had a mild seizure so we have increased his medication again. We have noticed in the last week that Michael is getting weaker. Today the only way he is able to communicate, in a way we understand, is to shake his head yes or no. Please pray for wisdom for Paul and me in the decisions we make. This Scripture has been very helpful to us today and reminded us of God's faithfulness amid our trials.

"When you pass through the waters, I will be with you; and through the rivers, they shall not overflow you. When you walk through the fire, you shall not be burned, nor shall the flame scorch you. For I am the LORD your God, the Holy One of Israel, your Savior" (Isaiah 43:2-3a).

Your prayers mean so much to us.

Journal —Sunday, December 4, 2011

My family came yesterday, Paul's today. My mom brought Michael a big stuffed snowman that we fastened to the stairway so he can see it from his bed! He has always loved stuffed animals.

Noticed that Michael's tongue was twitching again and he went catatonic. Mild seizure.

Journal—Monday, December 5, 2011

We decided to talk to the doctor about taking Michael off of all medication [because he was not able to swallow the pills and did not want an IV or feeding tube]. She thought that was fine, but we must be in agreement and not go back and forth if it gets rough. Lord, please if it be Your will, please take him quickly and peacefully.

Heard of a mom that passed away last night after a short battle with cancer. She was supposed to live one and a half to five years with chemo and radiation. God must have His timing for each of us. It can be so unpredictable though. Madame Guyon said: "What power there is in an accepted sorrow."

Caring Bridge Log—Wednesday, December 7, 2011

Michael appears much weaker today. He has not wanted anything to eat or drink because his stomach has been bothering him.

While praying with him this afternoon, Michael was able to tell me Jesus is here and then he also told me that Jesus was going to take him soon.

Please pray that Michael passes peacefully. Thank you for all your continued prayers.

Many have asked us if there is anything they can do for us or if we need anything. The only thing we really need right now is your prayers. We are very blessed to be surrounded by so many caring people.

Flashback

Michael seemed to have the simplicity of childlike faith. When he was about two years old, sitting in his booster seat, he told me, "Mom, want brother or a sister!"

I said, "Well, pray and ask God."

He folded his little hands and bowed his head and prayed, "God, want brother or sister."

After a moment of silence, he looked up, "God said, 'No.'" He just accepted the answer.

Caring Bridge Log—Friday, December 9, 2011

Recently I said I wouldn't have picked this time of the year to go through this. Ever since, in my heart, I have felt bad because I don't want to portray God as unkind or unloving. In fact, I have found His tender mercies are truly over all His works. The Christmas season has always been special to our family. We don't know exactly when Christ was born, but I love lighting the candles of our Advent wreath, reading scriptures of Jesus' coming, and singing carols that remind us of His love. This is a very comforting time of year especially when we can sit with Michael and look at the pretty lights on the Christmas tree and listen to Christmas songs.

The last two verses of the Christmas carol "Once in Royal David's City" are as follows:

> Jesus is our childhood pattern,
> Day by day like us He grew
> He was little, weak and helpless
> Tears and smiles like us He knew;
> And he feeleth for our sadness,
> And he shareth in our gladness.
>
> And our eyes at last shall see Him,
> Through His own redeeming love;
> For that Child so dear and gentle,
> Is our Lord in heaven above;
> And He leads his children on
> To the place where He is gone.

The hope of Heaven gives us great peace because Paul, Michael and I know we will all be together again forever.

Michael continues to have mild seizures and continues to grow weaker. We are waiting on God for His perfect timing to take him home. Your encouragement and prayers are a great blessing to us. Thank you so, so much!!

Caring Bridge Log—Saturday, December 10, 2011

Could you please pray for Michael tonight? He has had multiple minor seizures this evening, one right after another. Thankfully, he doesn't seem to be in much pain. Thank you very much for all your prayers.

Journal—Monday, December 12, 2011

Michael has been off all medication for a week. He continues to have minor seizures. One night was major. We gave him some medicine. It helped and he went to sleep. Dave and Dan were here for one of the seizures. It was eye opening. Tonight he had several minor ones. He has been very sweet though. He told me he does not remember the seizures.

Caring Bridge Log—Tuesday, December 13, 2011

A new picture of Michael is posted under the photos. It is his Christmas greeting to all of you!

Thank you for all your prayers for him. He periodically is still having mild seizures with leg cramps. He usually is not in pain though and we are thankful so many are praying for him. Most of the time he sleeps.

Journal—Saturday, December 17, 2011

Michael not talking at all. Very, very sweet though. Only liquids through dropper. Paul and I taking turns sleeping out here with him. Music for funeral done, but has Christmas song in it. I am wondering when—but God impressed on me this morning to act as though all has been taken care of. (Meaning, don't worry, live in peace about the timing.) Trust Him, know He is working behind the scenes and setting the stage for His perfect timing. Lord, I trust you to do above and beyond all that I can ever ask or think!

Caring Bridge Log—Tuesday, December 20, 2011

Paul and I want to thank everyone who has prayed and supported us through this year. We are amazed and overwhelmed by the kindness of those we know and those we don't know. Because of the great generosity of so many, all medical and final expenses for Michael have been met. Thanks to each of you for all the ways you have given and blessed our family.

Michael continues to grow weaker. Today he had a good day but this evening he had some pain in his right arm.

We plan to have a quiet Christmas at home. Thank you for your continued prayers. We are still waiting for God's perfect timing. We hope all of you have a blessed Christmas.

Insight Now

We are still amazed at such generosity!!!

Journal—Friday, December 23, 2011

Doctor is surprised he is doing so well.

Lord, please protect our marriage. Help me to lower my expectations and love Paul more and have a gentle and quiet spirit.

Insight Now

I don't remember now why I had written this. But, usually if I act or speak out of anger, I regret it. It is, at times, difficult to walk in love; especially when I am hurting and when I am tired. How I need to humble myself, not demand my own way, my own rights, and to focus on being a blessing to my husband. The women I most admire are those who have learned this. A cheerful, quiet, peaceful, helpful servant's heart is what I truly want. I think it is learned in the doing, when I don't feel that way. As I step out in obedience to the Lord, He changes my heart. What it takes is my yielding. That is the first step. "Love suffers long and is kind" (I Corinthians 13:4). A choice, not a feeling.

Therefore we do not lose heart. Even though our outward man is perishing, yet the inward man is being renewed day by day. For our light affliction, which is but for a moment, is working for us a far more exceeding and eternal weight of glory, while we do not look at the things which are seen, but at the things which are not seen. For the things which are seen are temporary, but the things which are not seen are eternal.

II CORINTHIANS 4:16-18

CHAPTER FIVE

Final Days

Caring Bridge Log—Wednesday, December 28, 2011

Michael had a quiet Christmas. He continues to have mild seizures and cramps in his arms and legs; but is not experiencing much pain and we are thankful for that. We continue to pray for God's timing. Michael is usually very peaceful and sleeps off and on throughout the day. The nights have been the most difficult due to lack of sleep. We would appreciate your prayers for peaceful nights.

Read this morning from F.B. Meyer:

> Stormy wind fulfilling his word. (Ps. 148:7,8) As it rushes through the forest, the hurricane tears down the rotten branches, and makes way for the new shoots of the spring.... Do not dread it, if you meet it rushing across the ocean and churning up the mighty billows on its way; know it to be your Father's strong servant, intent on fulfilling some errand on which it has been sent.

> Stormy winds not unseldom invade our lives. All had been so fair and blessed with us. The south wind, blowing softly, had led us to suppose that we might make for another harbour. But not long afterwards the tempestu-

ous Euroclydon beat down on us, bearing us far out of our course, and threatening us with destruction. But even under those circumstances, dare to trust. The stormy wind cannot separate you from God; for through its mad fury His angels will visit you, His care will surround you, His purpose will be fulfilled of bearing you onward, as the Apostle was borne toward Rome, with its opportunities of witness-bearing (Acts 27).

The great matter to remember is to run before the wind. Let its course be yours. Yield your will to God's will; and even though it bears you far out of your course, dare to believe that it is the quickest and best way of attaining the harbor which God has prepared. [36]

And then in *Joy and Strength* for December 28th:

Luke 18:17 (KJV) "Verily I say unto you, Whosoever shall not receive the Kingdom of God as a little child shall in no wise enter therein."

Childlikeness, in its Scripture sense, is a perfectness of trust, a resting in a Father's love, a being borne on in its power, living in it—it means a simplicity which resolves all into the one idea of lowly submissiveness to One in whom it lives; a buoyancy of spirit, which is a fountain of joy in itself, always ready to spring forth afresh brightly and happily to meet the claims of the present hour, not looking lingeringly back to the past, nor making plans independently, as of oneself, for the future; a resting contented in one's lot, whatever that lot may be; a singleness of intention; a pliancy, a yielding of the will, a forgetfulness of self in another's claims. To be thus childlike in the pure sense of such an ideal, is to be living in God, as one's Father, one's Preserver, one's Guide, felt to be a perpetual Presence and Providence.[37]

The key word for me in both is yielding! Not my way or my timing, but His. But who better to yield to than Jesus, who loves me and died to redeem me and gives me such hope for the future!

Caring Bridge Log—Monday, January 2, 2012

Michael has had a difficult night because of stomach troubles. When we ask him if he has any pain, he shakes his head no. He is resting peacefully and we are trying to keep him comfortable. Please continue to pray for God's timing in Michael's passing. Thank you for all your prayers.

Journal—Thursday, January 5, 2012

Made it through Christmas and New Year's. Over New Year's Michael sick to his stomach. Awful, painful to watch and made me feel sick. Nurse came later, all vital signs normal. Thought it might be end of life, but he is still coherent.

Paul and I cranky. Someone told me the divorce rate is very high when a child dies because spouses shut down. Asked friend to pray.

Part of Michael's smile returned. He is giving me hugs and then trying to punch me! Weather is unseasonably warm and very little snow this winter. Was sixty-five degrees today. Jogging when nice. Doctor thinks another week or two. Amazing.

I still have things to do. Yesterday, saw eagle soaring above me while I was jogging. Rise above it and rest. Many nights not enough sleep. Paul and I trade back and forth, but we get little and then we both still have to help him in the night.

Caring Bridge Log Saturday, January 7, 2012

After not speaking much at all, usually just nodding his head, Michael tried to speak in sentences today. Most of his speech is not understandable.

He continues to have stomach problems and mild seizures. The night time is the most difficult for all of us. Thank you for your continued prayers for our family and for God's timing.

Yesterday Paul and I read this poem by Annie Johnson Flint and it encouraged us:

> When you pass through the waters,
> Deep the waves may be and cold,
> But Jehovah is our refuge,
> And his promise is our hold;
> For the Lord Himself has said it,
> He, the faithful God and true;
> "When you come to the waters
> You will not go down, but THROUGH."
>
> Seas of sorrow, Seas of trial,
> Bitter anguish, fiercest pain,
> Rolling surges of temptation
> Sweeping over heart and brain…
> They will never overflow us

For we know His work is true;
All His waves and all His billows
He will lead us safely THROUGH.

Threatening breakers of destruction,
Doubt's insidious undertow,
Will not sink us, will not drag us
Out to ocean depths of woe;
For His promise will sustain us,
Praise the Lord, whose Word is true!
We will not go down, or under,
For He says, "You will pass THROUGH." [38]

Journal Saturday, January 7, 2012

Tonight, while I was laying next to Michael in his hospital bed, he and I prayed. Michael prayed brokenly for missionaries. Then said he wanted to go. He asked me to pray that Jesus would come and take him soon. His eyes were big and watching the ceiling while I prayed. His eyes moving back and forth across our vaulted ceiling and the loft.

I said, "What do you see?"

He whispered, "Angels."

I said, "What do they look like?"

He said, "They're wonderful!" [Looking very amazed when he said it.]

I asked him how many. No answer. I asked if more than two, he shook his head yes. I asked if more than five, he shook his head yes. I had the impression that there were more than he could count. I asked him if they were coming and going or if they were staying. He said yes to staying. Amazing. Whole new perspective!

Insight Now

I did not share this on Michael's Caring Bridge site because I didn't want people to be focused on angels.

Why did God allow Michael to see these? Why didn't I get to also? I don't know for sure. I wonder if God pulled back the curtain just to give Michael a glimpse of what was to come. My guess is that I didn't get to see them because I can become arrogant about things very easily!

The Bible tells us that angels protect God's people (Psalm 91).

If angels are observing my home, how much more God? My perspective should be that moment by moment all is said and done before the face of God. "The eyes of the Lord are in every place, keeping watch on the evil and the good" (Proverbs 15:3).

Caring Bridge Log—Tuesday, January 10, 2012

From my last update, I have had some questions so, I want to answer them. When I said Michael doesn't make sense sometimes, I don't mean he is not rational. He is still coherent and able to communicate his needs to us. He still prays with us and I can make out the names of the missionaries and families he is praying for.

The home health care nurse (who is so kind!) was here today for her weekly visit. Michael's vital signs remain the same, which is amazing because he is just taking fluids.

Thank you for your prayers for us for peaceful nights and for God's timing.

Caring Bridge Log—Friday, January 13, 2012

Could you please continue to pray for Michael? His legs and feet cramp up during his mild seizures and this is happening frequently. Please pray for peaceful nights, as they have been rare as of late. Thank you for remembering us in this way. Your prayers are so important to us at this time.

Journal—Tuesday, January 17, 2012

Last night received word from a friend that some people at a Pastors' Conference in Florida were praying for Michael. When I told Michael this, his face lit up and he was greatly encouraged. What a blessing!

Michael is mad at me for the moment. He went to hit me and missed and hit himself in the head. So sad when he won't receive love. And I just wanted to be with him. I long for these days to be over. Hard to stay in the present and accept when he is angry.

Caring Bridge Log—Thursday, January 19, 2012

Hebrews 6:18-19 "... it is impossible for God ever to prove false or deceive us, we who have fled [to Him] for refuge might have mighty indwelling strength and strong encouragement to grasp and hold fast the hope appointed for us and set before [us]. [Now] we have this [hope] as a sure and steadfast anchor of the soul [it cannot slip and it cannot break down under whoever steps out upon it—a hope]" Hebrews 6:18-19 (AMP).

Twice this week I have heard these verses being taught. I remember reading them when I was nineteen. As I shared them with my roommate, I wept because of the sense of hope and security they brought to my life.

Now in the midst of this storm which is raging longer than Paul and I ever thought or imagined possible, these words are a comfort again.

A commentary tells more about the anchor,

> In the catacombs of Rome, where Christians hid in times of persecution, one symbol can be seen more than any other: the anchor. No matter what storms come our way, we are anchored in the Word of God, in the promises He made. We have the sure hope that He will do what He says.... Be anchored in the immutable, unchangeable, sure and steadfast Word of God.[39]

I know I haven't updated Michael's condition lately. Truth is, he continues to have mild seizures with arm and leg cramps, and sometimes stomach trouble. Other than these symptoms, he has no major pain. He has grown weaker and is sleeping more, but the nights are still difficult at times. He has a sense of peace and calmness and when I ask him what he wants me to read to him, he wants me to read him the Bible.

Caring Bridge Log—Friday, January 20, 2012

Tonight Michael's breathing became slower and irregular. I talked to the doctor. He stated that Michael would probably pass in hours or days. When we told Michael he was going to be with Jesus soon, his face lit up and he smiled.

Please pray for God's timing. People have asked if we need anything. The only thing we really need is your prayers, which are so important to us right now.

Caring Bridge Log—Saturday, January 21, 2012

Last night was a long night. Michael's breathing is still slow and sporadic. We think he likes to prove the doctor wrong.

Thank you for continuing to hold us in your prayers. These verses and words from Fenelon in *Joy and Strength* were an encouragement to us this morning.

"Be of good courage, and He shall strengthen your heart, all ye that hope in the Lord" Psalm 31:24 (KJV).

"Lord, all my desire is before Thee" Psalm 38:9 (KJV).

When you find that weariness depresses or amusement distracts you, you will calmly turn with an untroubled spirit to your heavenly Father, who is always holding out His arms to you. You will look to Him for gladness and refreshment when depressed, for moderation and recollection when in good spirits, and you will find that He will never leave you to want. A trustful glance, a silent moment of the heart toward Him will renew your strength; and though you may often feel as if your soul were downcast and numb, whatever God calls you to do, He will give you power and courage to perform. Our heavenly Father, so far from ever overlooking us, is only waiting to find our hearts open, to pour into them the torrents of His grace. [40]

Caring Bridge Log Sunday, January 22, 2012

Just a quick note to let you know Michael's breathing has stayed about the same. However he has not been able to drink anything today and is becoming more unresponsive. Please continue to pray for God's timing and for wisdom in the decisions we have to make. Thank you for your continued prayers.

Caring Bridge Log Monday, January 23, 2012

The nurse was here this afternoon. Michael's blood pressure is lower, his pulse higher, breathing about the same, but his color is more pale. She also listened to his lungs and said they have fluid in them, probably from not being able to swallow as well. Her estimate time-wise was twenty-four to fourty-eight hours before he moves on to his next life.

Michael has been sleeping most of the day and the nights have been a little more peaceful. This was in our devotional this morning and we thought it was very timely. It is from *Morning and Evening* for January 23rd by C.H. Spurgeon.

> Christ was also chosen out of the people that he might know our wants and sympathize with us. "He was tempted in all points like as we are, yet without sin." In all our sorrows we have his sympathy. Temptation, pain, disappointment, weakness, weariness, poverty—he knows them all, for he has felt all. Remember this, Christian, and let it comfort thee. However difficult and painful thy road, it is marked by the footsteps of thy Savior; and even when thou reachest the dark valley of the shadow of death, and the deep waters of the swelling Jordan, thou wilt find his footprints there. In all places whithersoever we go, He has been our forerunner; each burden we have to carry, has once been laid on the shoulders of Immanuel.

His way was much rougher and darker than mine. Did

Christ, my Lord, suffer, and shall I repine?

Take courage! Royal feet have left a blood-red track upon
the road, and consecrated the thorny path forever. [41]

Caring Bridge Log Tuesday, January 24, 2012

This morning this was in our devotional, *Streams in the Desert*:

Delayed answers to prayer are not refusals. Many prayers are
received and recorded, yet underneath are the words, "My
time has not yet come." God has a fixed time and an ordained
purpose, and He who controls the limits of our lives also determines the time of our deliverance. [42]

I laughed when I read this this morning. God keeps reassuring me
that He has a plan!

Michael had a restful day, sleeping most of the time. His breathing is still sporadic but has lowered to about ten breaths per minute.
Amazingly, he is having very few mild seizures now, so we are sleeping
a little better at night. Thank you for all your prayers and for praying
for God's timing.

Journal Tuesday, January 24, 2012

Lord, help me to wait with a trusting, quiet, worshipful heart!

Caring Bridge Log Wednesday, January 25, 2012

Another perplexing day with Michael. Michael's breathing went
from eight breaths per minute this morning to thirty-three breaths per
minute this evening. His pulse is also high. The nurse indicated that his

breathing would eventually slow again. He is in a comatose state but appears to not have any pain and is resting comfortably. We are waiting on God for His timing.

Journal Wednesday, January 25, 2012

Read Leviticus 21 in a commentary:

> When tragedy strikes, when trials come, we'll either say, "This ought not to be. Poor me"—or we'll say, "This can be used for Your glory, so pour me, Lord. Pour me out to the people in need all around me."

> What did our great High Priest do in His time of tragedy, in His time of pain? Even as He hung on the Cross in agony, He ministered to a man beside Him, to a woman below Him, to the crowd around Him...

> Follow the example of Jesus. The best thing you can do when difficulties come your way is to go for it more than you ever have previously in giving out, in sharing with, in caring for those beside you and all around you. [43]

Insight Now

I share the following, not for you to feel sorry for me, but for you to know of God's great faithfulness and grace. As I write this, it is January 25, 2014. Two years from the hardest day of my life and I weep as I remember.

When I awoke on that morning, I was horrified at the condition of Michael's body. He was comatose, so frail, and so emaciated. I began to cry. What made it even harder, was I sensed evil mocking what death was doing to my son. I felt I could not go on. I felt I could not take care of him. Physically and emotionally I felt completely exhausted, even though I had just woken up. (We had been up in the night with him.) I went into our bedroom alone, knelt down and prayed. I asked God for grace to take care of him and for strength. My heart hurt so bad. God is so faithful. After praying, I rose and went and took care of Michael. And as I took care of him, God gave me the grace and strength and courage. I thought of Mary, the mother of Jesus. How her heart must have grieved to see the condition of her Son suffer through His passion, and die on the cross. So much worse than I was experiencing. And I thought of Jesus, how He chose to suffer for me. As I was caring for Michael, this verse came to mind: "Assuredly, I say to you, inasmuch as you did it to one of the least of these My brethren, you did it to Me" (Matthew 25:40). I had always wished I could have been at the cross when Jesus died. I wish I could have cared for Him. In some way, I felt I wasn't just caring for my beloved son, Michael, I was caring for God's beloved Son too.

I now know in the depth of my being, that no matter what I go through in the future, God's sustaining grace will be there to help me in my time of need. I can't imagine any suffering worse for me than what I went through that day. And God was there for me. I truly believe His heart hurt too.

Journal—Thursday, January 26, 2012

Dave came at 1:00 a.m. so Paul and I could sleep. [We asked him to come sit with Michael, because we needed sleep and we wanted someone to wake us if his breathing changed.] At 5:00 a.m., said breathing was shallow and more sighing. Dave left about 6:00 a.m. Then at 10:00 a.m., the clock was chiming, Michael started to sigh slowly several times. [I was kneeling next to Michael's bed and he was facing me, but his eyes were shut. Paul was on the other side. Friends had told us to be on the same side of the bed when he passed so he could see both of us. When his breathing changed, Paul came to the same side.] Michael's eyes opened, he nodded his chin at Paul and me and then he was gone. He was so sweet at the end. I thought of all the times he would wave at me from the steps of the house or run to the top gate to wave good-bye when I went somewhere.

Paul and I cried when he was gone. But it was also a time of worship and thanksgiving. I felt like a butterfly had wiggled out of it's cocoon. I think that is when his spirit left his body. Afterward, his body there, but his presence gone. He looked like my dad's high school picture.

The funeral home came later and very gently took his body. Paul said seven swans flew over our farm when he was outside—a rarity in Iowa, especially in the winter. Amazingly, seven is the number of completion and swans are symbolic of grace and peace. We went to tell my mom, then my brother and my dad. Then we went to eat. Beautiful flowers sent from Oregon—such a comfort.

It was so, so difficult to go home that night. As we came through the door, a huge wave of emptiness hit us. The house was void. An empty hospital bed sat in our living room. Later, I opened Paul's anniversary card to me. It said, the best was yet to be. I cried. He meant that the best would be being together again in Heaven with Michael. But I had to fight a negative thought that entered my mind—the rest of my life would be futile, no purpose, the best here was over. This was a lie to lead me to despair. I had heard it before. I had seen it before in the lives of others. I would not make any agreement with it. God's promise is to give me a "future and a hope." A future here on earth and the hope of Heaven. I told Paul about the lie and he prayed with me.

Caring Bridge Log Thursday, January 26, 2012

Today, Thursday, January 26, at 10:00 a.m., Michael went to be with his Lord and Savior, Jesus Christ, his Good Shepherd! He passed peacefully from this life to the next.

Amazingly, today is our twenty-first wedding anniversary, and we truly have no greater joy than to know that our son walks in truth and is probably running all over Heaven (III John 4)!

We will post more details later. In the interim, we would appreciate your prayers for all the decisions we have to make about his funeral service. Thank you for all your offers to help. But the only thing we really need is your prayers. Paul and I are going into seclusion for a while.

Thank you for everything!

God Bless Each of YOU!!!

Insight Now

I heard that someone upon hearing of Michael's passing, made the comment, "God made a mistake." God is too big to ever make a mistake.

Edith Schaeffer, in her book *Affliction*, says about God and suffering:

We do know that our God who is sovereign does not have "chance" to contend with. He has told us that He is able to take whatever has taken place and to work together all things for the good of those who are His children. . . However, that does not eliminate the fact that we simply do not know what flow of factors brought about the accident, the illness, the fire, the earthquakes, the storm, and the combination of events in the middle of it all. Our assurance as children of the Living God is that He is able to bring beauty from ashes and to give the "oil of joy" for the spirit of mourning (see Isaiah 61:3). And in addition, He refines, purifies, proves, and causes to grow in us something very precious and lasting in our attitudes toward Him and in our actions to other human beings. As we turn to Him in our affliction and ask for help, He does not allow our affliction to be "wasted." . . .There is a "coming through," with a shinier, more gleaming sheen on our surface. We have the possibility during the hard time to have skimmed off more of the specks and scum which are hindering the more beautiful reality of love, joy, peace, long-suffering, and meekness.[44]

Why the suffering? This from *Streams in the Desert*, December 2:

Suffering is a wonderful fertilizer for the roots of character. The great objective of this life is character, for it is the only thing we can carry with us into eternity. And gaining as much of the highest character possible is the purpose of our trials.[45]

Caring Bridge Log—Friday, January 27, 2012

We want each of you to know that Michael passed very peacefully. His breathing had not slowed until about five minutes before he passed. He sighed several times slowly and then opened his eyes. Paul and I were kneeling together next to his bed. He nodded his head to say goodbye and then he was gone. He was so sweet as he gave us this sign of his leaving. This was an answer to my prayers, that we would both be there with him and be able to say goodbye.

Paul and I are so thankful for all the prayers. Yesterday was a difficult day. This morning my first thought was Michael is in Heaven with Jesus, and that is very comforting!!!

Caring Bridge Log—Friday, January 27, 2012

The Obituary of Michael Moede

With his parents by his side, Michael Christopher Gilchrist Moede, 13, went to be with his Good Shepherd on Thursday, January 26, 2012. Funeral services will be 1:00 p.m. Saturday, February 4, 2012, at First Church of the Open Bible, 2200 Beaver Avenue, with burial following at North River Cemetery, rural Norwalk. A visitation will be from 4:00 p.m. to 8:00 p.m., Friday, February 3, 2012, at the church.

Michael loved the Lord Jesus Christ. He was homeschooled his whole life and greatly enjoyed God's creation. He enjoyed hunting, fishing, hiking, painting, drawing and playing the piano.

Michael is survived by his father and mother, Paul and Joni Moede; his maternal grandparents, Ken Gilchrist and Elnor Gilchrist; his caring aunts and uncles, Nancy and Donald Wright, David and Sue Moede, Dan and Michelle Moede, Ralph and Katie Lane, KJ and Joni Gilchrist, Vicky and Rodger McKim and many extended family members and friends. He was preceded in death by his paternal grandparents, Paul F. Moede, Jr., and Wanda Smith. [46]

Caring Bridge Log Friday, January 27, 2012

This tribute was written by Ben Dorin on his blog. A young man who had taken an interest in Michael.

Dearly Beloved, please bear with me as I tell you a story of courage...

Today, I and many others were given an incredible example of courage. There was no knight in shining armor, no soldier with the medal of honor around his neck, no earthly foe that had been vanquished. There weren't thousands of people waiting to welcome home a hero. The President was not waiting to congratulate a veteran. No, the courage I have seen today is altogether different. No earthly battle had been fought, no earthly victory had been won. Rather, it was a spiritual battle that was fought, and it was an eternal victory that was won.

Now, whereas there was no multitude of people, no welcoming parade, there was an innumerable number of angels welcoming home a conquering warrior. There was a tender father ushering His servant into His rest.

Today, a young man scarcely thirteen years of age, went home to be with the Lord. Over the past year, I have witnessed this young man look at death in the face and stand immovable. He could boldly look at death and proclaim, "Oh death where is your sting; oh grave, where is your victory." He could lift his eyes to heaven and utter, "I know that if this earthly tabernacle be destroyed, I have a building not made with hands, eternal in the heavens." He could proudly proclaim, "I know in whom I have believed and am persuaded that He is able to keep that which I have committed unto Him against that day." This young man met death, he crossed the Jordan, he took His final journey and now He sits whole in the presence of the Lord. This is courage.

This young man died of a very progressive form of brain cancer. At the time of diagnosis, he was given six months to live. However, he lived approximately four months beyond the deadline. He brought cheer and happiness to all who knew him. And whereas he lost most bodily function before death due to the cancer, this young man is now whole, complete, and perfect in the presence of his Lord.

Take heed, brethren. Take heed. We all fade as the grass. It is appointed for everyone to die. We have been given an example of courage today. Let this serve as a wake up call to redeem the time we have been given.

Furthermore, I want to ask you: Are you living life for God or for you? Will you hear the words: "Well done good and faithful servant?" Are you living courageously? Are you fighting the fight? Brethren, "Lay aside the sin that doth so easily besets you and run with patience the race that is set before you."

This young man, fought and won. He ran and finished his course. He courageously met death. He followed after the Lord Jesus Christ that conquered death for us. Take heart. Take heart! He has now joined the cloud of witnesses pointing you to heaven. Run the race.

Michael Moede
Passed Away at thirteen years of age,
January 26,
In the year of our Lord,
2012

What is courage my dear lad
But having the strength to stand
What is courage but to have
An unwavering hand.

Courage proudly looks at death
And does not affright
Courage gladly gives up breath
And does not take flight.

Soli Deo Gloria [47]

Caring Bridge Log—Tuesday, January 31, 2012

Paul and I want everyone to know they are welcome at Michael's visitation and funeral service. Many of you, even though we have never met, have been praying for our family and we would be honored to have you with us, celebrating Michael's life. Please feel welcome—we would love to meet you!

Thanks to each of you for your prayers. We are thankful we are surrounded by so many caring, helpful people! Please pray for the visitation and service that all who come will experience God's peace and comfort.

Caring Bridge Log—Wednesday, February 1, 2012

Would you please pray about the weather for Friday night and Saturday? The forecasters are expecting freezing rain and maybe six inches of snow from Friday into Saturday. We do not want anyone hindered from coming to the visitation and funeral because of the weather.

Truly, truly, I say to you, unless a grain of wheat

falls into the earth and dies, it remains alone; but

if it dies, it bears much fruit.

JOHN 12:24 (NASB)

CHAPTER SIX

The Funeral

This is the transcript of what Paul and I shared at Michael's funeral and also Michael's message. I share them here because we feel so impressed that people understand God's heart about Michael's passing.

Paul's Comments at Michael's Funeral

[After thanking everyone for everything.]

I heard that some of Michael's friends were feeling a little angry at God for the way things turned out with him. I would just want to say to them, the facts aren't all in on Michael, on why this happened to him. In fact, if we just looked at the bad things that happened to Jesus, if that's all we knew about, if we didn't know why, we didn't know the reason but just knew that He was beat up, and spit on and cursed and had a crown of thorns jammed on His head, and was whipped until he was raw, and then nailed to a cross—if that's all we knew, if we knew nothing else—then we would think God is really not a very nice God. But we do know the rest of the story with Jesus. That it was for a purpose, and that it was for the redemption, the redemption of all mankind. And because we know that, because we know the rest of the story with Jesus, we know that He is a good God. He is a loving God, all the time. He is perfect in all His ways. The facts aren't all in on Michael, but because of what we know about Jesus, I am sure that if we knew the rest of the story with Michael, we would say, "Wow, He's a great God!" So, don't be angry with God. He loves us. He is on our side. He did everything to save us. He came to earth, the most tremendous condescension ever. He died for us. He gave us His blood to redeem us.

My Comments at Michael's Funeral

[The week of Michael's passing, we heard two young people in our community had committed suicide. The passing of these young people was on my heart, as well as Michael's young friends, who were wondering why God did not answer their prayers and heal Michael this side of Heaven.]

When someone dies, it can be hard to understand, especially someone so young. And it can put fear in our hearts. What if this happens to me or someone I love? Several years ago, a woman I knew died, passed from this life. When she passed, I questioned God. "Why? Her family needs her. Why?" And God did not answer my questions, but He reminded me of this verse, Isaiah 55:8–9. "'For My thoughts are not your thoughts, nor are your ways My ways,' says the Lord. 'For as the heavens are higher than the earth, so are My ways higher than your ways, and My thoughts than your thoughts.'"

And it is kind of like this needlework picture. On the back side it is messy, there are a lot of loose ends and we don't see the picture clearly. Sometimes, that is what my life is like. I wonder what is happening. But God, He is the master weaver. He sees the whole thing and He is weaving something beautiful in our lives. And He determines the length of each thread and how it is woven. The thought that He sees the whole picture, helps me greatly.

Psalm 145:9 says, "The Lord is good to all, and His tender mercies are over all His works." That helps me. The verse Romans 8:28 says, "And we know that all things work together for good to those who love God, to those who are the called according to His purpose."

Sometimes though, I've hit bumps in the road, like what we have been through with Michael—and it is difficult. But what helps me most of all is to look at the cross. And when I look at the cross, I know that Jesus gave everything for me and I know I can trust Him because He has a heart of love. In Hebrews 12:1–2 it says, "...let us run with endurance the race that is set before us, looking unto Jesus, the author and finisher of our faith...." Jesus ran the race, and He will be there at the finish line. But the wonderful thing about Jesus is, He is with us everyday as our coach in the race. And He has a set race for each one of us. What we have been through, other people may not go through. God has something different for each one of us on our race. And He will give us His grace for whatever our race entails. He won't ask us to run a marathon if we're not trained for it. He prepares us. He's preparing us for Heaven. He will help us.

I love what Isaiah 43:2 says, "When you pass through the waters, I will be with you...."

Psalm 91:15 "I will be with him in trouble; I will deliver him...."

Matthew 28:20 "Lo, I am with you always, even to the end...."

Hebrews 13:5 "I will never leave you nor forsake you...."

Some people though, have dropped out of the race. I don't want that to happen to anyone. God has a plan for each one of us. Jeremiah 29:11 (NIV) "'For I know the plans I have for you,' declares the Lord, 'plans to prosper you and not to harm you, plans to give you hope and a future.'" There is never a reason for us to drop out of the race, He is with us and will help us. Above all in this race, He will give us peace and courage.

One of Michael's favorite verses that he memorized when he was three or four years old is Joshua 1:9, "Be strong and of good courage; do not be afraid, nor be dismayed, for the Lord your God is with you wherever you go."

And when we have Jesus, when we have that relationship with Him and Him as our coach, and we can hold onto His promises, that gives us great peace—peace that passes all understanding.

Michael's Message

[This was recorded when Michael was still able to talk fairly well.]

Hi! My name is Michael Moede and if you are watching this video, then I have probably croaked. Right now as we are filming, I feel pretty good and am not in any pain, but the cancer has made it hard for me to smile, so if I look grumpy, that's why. I just want to take a few moments and tell you some things.

The Bible says that life is like a vapor, we're here one moment and gone the next. But where do we go? That depends on your choice. I've got some good news and some bad news. The good news is that "God so loved the world that He gave His only begotten Son, that whoever believes in Him should not perish but have everlasting life. For God did not send His Son into the world to condemn the world, but that the world through Him might be saved. He who believes in Him is not condemned; but he who does not believe is condemned already, because he has not believed in the name of the only begotten Son of God." John 3:16-18.

We can live with God forever in Heaven or we can be separated from Him forever. To live with God forever in Heaven we must become holy for God is holy. But we have all sinned. We need what my friend, Pastor Jon Courson, calls the "great switcheroo." Jesus left Heaven, came to Earth as God in flesh, lived a perfect sinless life, then died on the cross for our sins and then rose again three day later. So, He took our sin and will give us His righteousness if we repent of our sin and will accept His free gift. The Bible says that God is not willing that any should perish but that all should come to repentance. To repent means to turn away from sin.

I ask you today, if you are not sure where you will spend eternity will you join me? Will you turn away from sin and turn toward Jesus?

If you are a Christian, are you ready to go to Heaven? When you stand before God and give an account of your life, how will you do? What are you investing your life in—things of this earth or things of Heaven? Are you investing in His kingdom not because you have to but because you want to? Because God gave everything for you. Join me in Heaven. Join me in hearing, "Well done good and faithful servant, enter now into the joy of the Lord."

And thank you to those of you who have given me cards, and prayed for me, and given gifts. They're all very encouraging to me. Thank you.

And if you're grieving that I'm dead, don't! Because if I were in Hawaii, you wouldn't be so sad. But here I am in Heaven, a lot better than Hawaii. See ya!

Caring Bridge Log Wednesday, February 8, 2012

Thank you to each of you who prayed for us last week, who came to the visitation or to the funeral service. We felt so encouraged and strengthened by your prayers, presence, outpourings of love and hugs!!! Even the day of the funeral, I had such joy in my heart. Yes, I miss Michael, but I am so thankful he ran his race well, finished well and now is with Jesus. To God be all the glory!!!

Many have commented about not being able to attend due to the weather. Our nephew, Josh, recorded the service. It is viewable at www.michaelsfinalmessage.com.

We are so thankful for Josh's help and could not have done the service without him. And we are thankful that he helped us record Michael's message while Michael was still able to talk.

The devotional from *Streams in the Desert* was so encouraging Monday morning. It says:

> "He turned the sea into dry land; they went through the flood on foot: there did we rejoice in him" (Psalm 66:6, KJV).

> It is a profound statement, "through the waters" the very place where we might have expected nothing but trembling, terror, anguish and dismay the children of Israel stopped to "rejoice in him"!

> How many of us can relate to this experience? Who of us, right in the midst of our time of distress and sadness, have been able to triumph and rejoice as the Israelites did?

How close God is to us through His promises, and how brightly those promises shine! Yet during times of prosperity, we lose sight of their brilliance. In the way the sun at noon hides the stars from sight, His promises become indiscernible. But when night falls—the deep, dark night of sorrow—a host of stars begin to shine, bringing forth God's blessed constellations of hope, and promises of comfort from His Word. . .

It was during a dark time of loneliness and exile that John had the glorious vision of his Redeemer. Many of us today have our "Isle of Patmos," which produces the brightest memories of God's enduring presence, uplifting grace, and love in spite of solitude and sadness.

How many travelers today, still passing through these Red Seas and Jordans of earthly affliction, will be able to look back from eternity, filled with memories of God's great goodness and say, "We passed through the waters on foot." And yet, even in these dark experiences, with waves surging all around, we stopped and said, "Let us rejoice in him!" [48]

It is so true that in the dark night, His promises shine forth and give such hope!

Thank you for everything! We are so blessed and God is so good and so faithful!!!

Weeping may endure for a night,

But joy comes in the morning.

PSALM 30:5

CHAPTER SEVEN

Lessons Learned Through Grief

Since Michael's passing, there are lessons I have learned and am still learning on this journey. There were also some very special things that happened that just amaze my heart. I share them with you in the hope that they will encourage you through whatever storms you face, and show once again the graciousness of God.

Pouring Out My Heart

The first few weeks after Michael passed were the most difficult for me. I continued my daily routine. I rose early, sat at the kitchen table, read my Bible and prayed. Through the bay window I watched the sunrise. And I would cry. I would pour out my heart to the Lord. But what I began to notice was a sinking feeling that would start to come over me. I felt like I was sinking into quicksand from which I would not be able to escape. At times, the painful thoughts would pile one on top of another. This happened, and then this happened, and then this.... So, I began to try to pray prayers of thanksgiving after my cry. I would cry out the pain, but then I would choose, not a feeling—a choice—to thank God for ways in which He was working in my life. This helped me immensely! It helped keep me out of self-pity, out of utter desolation and despair. I would thank God that Michael's message was out on YouTube and then pray that He would use it for His glory. So, the habit of crying out the pain and then giving thanks kept me from sinking into the quicksand of despair.

About two months before Michael's diagnosis, a friend gave me the book *Choosing Gratitude* by Nancy Leigh DeMoss. It was so timely for me to read before our storm began. She writes:

> I have seen how a lack of gratitude manifests itself in fretting, complaining, and resenting—whether within the confines of my own thoughts or, worse yet, through venting those thoughts to others. But in those moments when I have found myself gasping for air, feeling that I was going under, I've discovered that gratitude truly is my life preserver. Even in the most turbulent waters, choosing gratitude rescues me from myself and my runaway emotions. It buoys me on the grace of God and keeps me from drowning in what otherwise would be my natural bent toward doubt, negativity, discouragement, and anxiety. [49]

Now this may seem like a Pollyannaish attitude, but it is a command in scripture. "... giving thanks always for all things to God the Father in the name of our Lord Jesus Christ" (Ephesians 5:20). And after walking through the pain I have been through, I can honestly say that it is one of the most helpful things to me. Spending time worshiping God and being in His presence are also extremely helpful.

Going On With Life

A second thing that helped me was what I heard Elisabeth Elliot teach on the radio years ago, "Do the next thing!" So, daily I would ask God to show me what He had for me that day. My job as Michael's homeschool teacher was over. (He joked once during his illness, that I had been fired!) But there were lots of practical things that I needed to do—daily cooking, cleaning, laundry, and many, many thank you notes. I did these a little at a time and it took me a year. I wanted to write a personal note to each person who had blessed us before, during and after Michael's passing. We also wanted to pass on to other home-school families many of Michael's books. Going through Michael's things and deciding what Paul and I wanted to pass on to others and what we did not want to part with was hard at times. If I began to cry, I would cry it out and then go work on something else for a while. As time has gone on, we have given away more and kept less. But it has become easier to give and a blessing to give to those who knew Michael and appreciate something that was his.

When I read *Streams in the Desert*, March 11, about a month after the funeral, the Lord impressed on my heart to not stay stuck in the past. It says:

> Yesterday, you experienced a great sorrow, and now your home seems empty. Your first impulse is to give up and to sit down in despair amid your dashed hopes. Yet you must defy that temptation, for you are at the front line of battle, and the crisis is at hand. Faltering even one moment would put God's interest at risk. Other lives will be harmed by

your hesitation, and His work will suffer if you simply fold your hands. You must not linger at this point, even to indulge your grief.

A famous general once related this sorrowful story from his own wartime experience. His son was the lieutenant of an artillery unit, and an assault was in progress. As the father led his division in a charge, pressing on across the battlefield, suddenly his eye caught sight of a dead artillery officer lying right before him. Just a glance told him it was his son. The general's fatherly impulse was to kneel by the body of his beloved son and express his grief, but the duty of the moment demanded he press on with his charge. So, after quickly kissing his dead son, he hurried away, leading his command in the assault.

Weeping inconsolably beside a grave will never bring back the treasure of a lost love, nor can any blessing come from such great sadness. Sorrow causes deep scars, and indelibly writes its story on the suffering heart. We never completely recover from our greatest griefs and are never exactly the same after having passed through them. Yet sorrow that is endured in the right spirit impacts our growth favorably and brings us a greater sense of compassion for others. Indeed, those who have no scars of sorrow or suffering upon them are poor. "The joy set before" (Heb. 12:2) us should shine on our griefs just as the sun shines through the clouds, making them radiant. God has ordained our truest and richest comfort to be found by pressing on toward the goal. Sitting down and brooding over our sorrow deepens the darkness surrounding us, allowing it to creep into our heart. And soon our strength has changed to weakness. But if we will turn from the gloom and remain faithful to the calling of God, the light will shine again and we will grow stronger. [50]

Now, I am not saying don't take time to grieve. There seem to be two extremes. We can stay so busy that we don't grieve, or we can get stuck in the grief and not go on with our lives. Although, I am not in a military battle and I'm not on the front lines, there is a spiritual battle taking place. Each person in the body of Christ has a place to fill in that battle and only they can fulfill their part. Life is a vapor (James 4:14) and we are called to redeem the time (Ephesians 5:16). So, if I am living in light of eternity, wanting to do all I can do for the One who loves me because I only have one life to give Him, I want to give everything! I want to be available at every moment for every purpose of His all for His glory. "... for all things come from You, and of Your own we have given You" (I Chronicles 29:14).

I do not want to stay stuck in the past. I will not forget it, and when triggered, I will still probably cry, but I refuse to keep focused on the past. It helps me so much to not stuff my heart—keeping it from crying when it is hurting. Crying is a release of my grief and there are tons of instances of it in the Bible. So, when I am hurting, I cry, usually when I am alone. There have been times in church while worshiping the Lord or times when talking with friends about Michael that I have wept. To me, crying is like a pressure valve on my heart. If the grief pressure builds up, I cry it out. Then I feel better and I can refocus on the present. But I try very hard to not cry for the wrong reasons: having others feel sorry for me, making it all about me, or indulging in self-pity; all of which make God look like He is heartless. And I know from looking at the cross, that He is the exact opposite of heartless!

Marital Stress

After Michael passed, someone sent me the book, *Don't Waste Your Sorrows*. In it, I found one of the best explanations about how to view marriage:

> There may be exceptions, but most newlyweds have not yet learned the true meaning of unselfishness. They may be saved, sanctified, or filled with the Holy Spirit, and still be unconsciously self-centered. One of God's main purposes in ordaining marriage and the home is not primarily for pleasure, as is ordinarily supposed, but to decentralize the self, to teach agape love. The stresses of marriage and the home are designed to produce brokenness, to wean one from self-centeredness, and to produce the graces of sacrificial love and gentleness.[51]

So, now I am learning to go to the Lord and let Him fill my heart with His love, and then love my husband without expectations. Sometimes this means dying to self, to the things that I think I need or want. But the good that has come from this is that my husband is released from my expectations, making a happier husband; and my roots have grown deeper in the love of Jesus. For many years, I had tried to live unselfishly, but had not learned to turn to God with my needs. Then I read a book called *The Perfect Love*, by Ruth Myers. She explained how she learned to let God be what she needed:

> The most important truth in my life is that God wants me to know Him in intimate, personal experience. Yes, He wants me to know the true concepts about Him in His Word. But He wants me to take each of those concepts and allow Him to be that to me in personal experience.... Be to me what You are. You are my best love—be that to me now, for I need that today. You are the water of life—be that to me at this time, because my soul is thirsty. Here's where praise comes in, turning our eyes to what He is and giving Him thanks and praise. Then our experience begins to line up with these truths, and He begins to move in with a growing reality of Himself. [52]

This has been so helpful to me. It is not a feeling, it is just a trust, an expectation that as I turn to Him, He will be to me what I need.

Support System

During Michael's illness and over the last few years, the body of Christ as a whole and our local church have been such a blessing to us on this journey. I cannot even begin to count the times their reaching out to us has been a healing balm to our hurting hearts. Caring friends were so helpful! Broken people are best able to support those who are hurting. They know—they have been there. Isolating is not good. At the time of and years following Michael's passing, I don't know what would have happened to us if we had not had the love, prayers, and support of so many people.

Extending Grace

When people have said things that have not been helpful, I am learning to extend grace as I have had grace extended to me by my Savior. How many times have I said the wrong thing, especially to someone who is hurting and I had no clue what they were going through? So, I continue to learn to minimize the situation (don't make a big deal of it), and pray (pray for them and for myself to respond graciously). And as one of my mentors tells me in her southern accent, "Don't take up an offense!"

Guilt and Regrets

Feelings of guilt and regret surfaced often. When these thoughts of the past seem to bombard me, I realize what I must do. If I have not asked God's forgiveness, I confess my sin and ask His forgiveness and thank Him for it. I remember that Michael has forgiven me. And as a dear friend told me, "He is not up there in Heaven holding a grudge toward you!" Before he passed, I had asked his forgiveness for all my failings and he sweetly forgave me. Then, I remind myself of a gift someone gave me at Michael's funeral. It is a beautiful bird holding a banner that says, "Peace and love in every memory." It hangs on the knob of my desk to this day. It is a reminder to me to think on the good memories and not dwell on the negative. Philippians 4:8 says:

"Finally, brethren, whatever things are true, whatever things are noble, whatever things are just, whatever things are pure, whatever things are lovely, whatever things are of good report, if there is any virtue and if there is anything praiseworthy—meditate on these things."

Holidays and Special Days

Losing a loved one is very hard. Losing a child is very hard. We don't expect them to pass from this life before we do. Holidays can compound the pain. Memories come flooding back. I remember the difficulties our first Christmas without Michael. While Christmas shopping, I walked into a store and saw a sign that read, "The laughter of a child is the light of the home." I burst into tears and could hardly make it out of the store fast enough. Our home had seemed so silent, so much quieter than before. God was so gracious though. In His sovereign timing, our nephew and his wife had their first child the same month Michael passed and they came to my sister's that first Christmas that we were without our son. No one will ever replace Michael in our hearts, but this was a new life to celebrate. It made the Christmas season more bearable. I have found that even though the holidays are different now, God has new things for us.

On the anniversary of Michael passing, which is also our wedding anniversary, we go to the cemetery. We go other times during the year, but especially then. Our wedding anniversary has taken on a more somber tone. Our love has deepened, though. There is a peace and contentment in our lives.

About a month after Michael's funeral, I watched two great blue herons standing next to each other on a limb high up in a sycamore tree. It was a cold, cloudy day. The wind was howling. But those two heron were perched side by side with their backs to the wind. And no matter how shaken they were on that limb, they endured it together. That picture spoke volumes to my heart—perseverance, determination, no matter what.

Whenever there are family gatherings now, it is very obvious to Paul and me that someone is missing, a part of us has gone before us, and he is missed greatly. I think my longing for Heaven has increased exponentially! The hope of Heaven is such a comfort. It will not always be this way. Soon we will see our Savior and our son.

Reaching Out

Which leads into my next topic, reaching out to those who are hurting, not just during the holidays, but daily being attentive to the needs around me. My heart aches for others now when I hear they are going through similar difficulties. Reaching out to them, not staying in my turtle shell, is an opportunity for me to show the love of Christ. I must reach out to reflect His love, and not focus on myself or what I have been through. II Corinthians 1:3-5 says,

> Blessed be the God and Father of our Lord Jesus Christ, the Father of mercies and God of all comfort, who comforts us in all our tribulation, that we may be able to comfort those who are in any trouble, with the comfort with which we ourselves are comforted by God. For as the sufferings of Christ abound in us, so our consolation also abounds through Christ.

I ask God to comfort me and then direct me in how to respond to those who are hurting.

Hang on to the Promises of God

In September 2012, I was listening to a radio program called *Pastor's Perspective*. Pastor Chuck Smith was the host and Pastor Greg Laurie was on the air with him that day answering questions from callers. I called in with the question, "How do I grieve rightly?" I explained that Michael was in Heaven. They were so helpful. Pastor Chuck talked about how when his father and brother were killed in a plane crash, initially the waves of grief were intense and frequent. He told me they would get less intense and less frequent in time. Pastor Greg, whose son was killed in a car accident, explained a great analogy to me. He talked about how a good surfer has his surf board tethered to his ankle. When a big wave hits him, he falls off the board and looses all perspective. But if he holds onto the tether, it leads him back to the surface and to his board. So, when the storms of life hit, and I feel like I'm going under, I need to hang on to the promises of God. The Bible is my tether and God's promises will help me regain my perspective. Both pastors encouraged me to pour out my heart to the Lord and to remember that everyone grieves differently.

These are some of my favorite promises that I have prayed and thanked God for:

"Though the fig tree may not blossom, nor fruit be on the vines; though the labor of the olive may fail, and the fields yield no food; though the flock may be cut off from the fold, and there be no herd in the stalls—yet I will rejoice in the Lord, I will joy in the God of my salvation" (Habakkuk 3:17-18).

"There is no one like the God of Jeshurun, Who rides the heavens to help you, and in His excellency on the clouds. The eternal God is your refuge, and underneath are the everlasting arms" (Deuteronomy 33:26-27).

"As for God, His way is perfect; the word of the Lord is proven; He is a shield to all who trust in Him. For who is God, except the Lord? And who is a rock, except our God? It is God who arms me with strength, and makes my way perfect" (Psalm 18:30-32).

"Fear not, for I am with you; be not dismayed, for I am your God. I will strengthen you, yes, I will help you, I will uphold you with My righteous right hand" (Isaiah 41:10).

The Heavenly Jerusalem

The last experience I want to share is about Heaven and God's amazing timing. On Mother's Day, 2013, I flew to Los Angles, and then the next day, which was Michael's birthday, I boarded a plane bound for Israel. Years ago, I had dreamed of going to Israel, and the dream came true! It was a fabulous trip and I learned so much! God orchestrated an event that gave me a clearer picture of Heaven. On a Thursday, our tour group was in the old city of Jerusalem having lunch at an outdoor cafe. All of sudden there was music, and clapping, and a rejoicing parade of friends and family. They were parading a young Jewish boy under a canopy that had four poles, and four young boys each held one of the four poles. The people were smiling and so happy for this young boy walking under the canopy. Our tour guide explained that around the time that a Jewish boy turns thirteen, it is a very special day, his bar mitzvah. Friends and family join in celebrating the young boy coming of age. It was a Thursday, Michael passed on a Thursday.

I felt compelled to ask our guide, "What happens at 10:00 a.m. on the day of the bar mitzvah?"

He said, "At 10:00 a.m., the boy goes into the temple and reads from the Torah for the first time and he becomes a man."

At the age of thirteen, on a Thursday, Michael passed as our clock was chiming 10:00 a.m. I was watching all this from the earthly Jerusalem. Michael was in the Heavenly Jerusalem. Hebrews 12:22–23 says,

> But you have come to Mount Zion and to they city of the living God, the heavenly Jerusalem, to an innumerable company of angels, to the general assembly and church of the firstborn who are registered in heaven, to God the Judge of all, to the spirits of just men made perfect....

I felt so close to Michael, even though we were in two different places. And it made me wonder, was there a celebration for him when he entered Heaven? I think there was!

Living in Light of Eternity

In closing, I want to tell you as a mom, my greatest joy is knowing that Michael is in Heaven and that he finished his race well. All the material things, time, and sacrifices made to be with our son and train this young life for eternity, were worth it. Yes, it is God's grace at work, but we have a choice to yield to Him or to make other things our priority. Whatever He asks of us, it is for a great reason, and for a great purpose, and we will not regret whatever sacrifices we make. I wonder, will we know the extent of the repercussions of our actions when we stand before God? His word tells us, "whatever a man sows, that he will also reap" (Galatians 6:7).

Randy Alcorn reminds us in his excellent book, *Heaven*:

> Heaven should affect our activities and ambitions, our rec-

reation and friendships, and the way we spend our money and time. If I believe I'll spend eternity in a world of unending beauty and adventure, will I be content to spend all my evenings staring at game shows, sitcoms, and ball games? Even if I keep my eyes off of impurities, how much time will I want to invest in what doesn't matter? What will last forever? God's Word. People. Spending time in God's Word and investing in people will pay off in eternity and bring me joy and perspective now. [53]

My life verse, that I chose when I was a new Christian, is John 12:24 (NASB) "Unless a grain of wheat falls into the earth and dies, it remains by itself alone; but if it dies, it bears much fruit." Michael was my grain of wheat. As his mom, a wretch saved by amazing grace, I am thankful for all the way the Lord has led us. And I am even more thankful for where He is leading us—Heaven!

To watch Michael's message, or to learn more about knowing Jesus Christ, you can go to: www.michaelsfinalmessage.com

End Notes

1. *Searchlight* radio program can be found at www.joncourson.com.

2. James Hinton, quoted in *Joy and Strength*, comp. Mary Wilder Tileston (Minneapolis, MN: World Wide Publications, 1986), March 4.

3. Betty Scott Stam's prayer, www.sermonindex.net, Christian Quotes on Obedience, accessed February 13, 2016.

4. T. T. Carter, quoted in *Joy and Strength*, comp. Mary Wilder Tileston (Minneapolis, MN: World Wide Publications, 1986), March 25.

5. Peter J. Marshall, Jr. and David B. Manuel, Jr., *The Light and the Glory* (Grand Rapids, MI: Baker Book House Company, 1977), 245-246.

6. We are indebted to Steve and Carolyn Poetzl for this idea.

7. *The Lord of the Rings: The Fellowship of the Ring*, directed by Peter Jackson (New Line Productions, Inc., 2001).

8. Elisabeth Elliot, *Shadow of the Almighty: The Life & Testament of Jim Elliot* (New York, NY: HarperCollins Publishers, 1979), 184

9. Jon Courson, *Jon Courson's Application Commentary, Old Testament, Volume 1: Genesis–Job* (Nashville, TN: Thomas Nelson, Inc., 2005), 850.

10. W. E. Cule, *Sir Knight of the Splendid Way* (Mount Morris, NY: Lamplighter Publishing, 2002), inside back cover.

11. F. B Meyer, *Our Daily Homily*, Psalm 66:10.

12. Jon Courson, *A Future and a Hope; Sermons of Comfort in Seasons of Confusion* (Santa Ana, CA: Calvary Chapel Publishing, 2006), 163.

13. Hannah Whitall Smith, quoted in *Joy and Strength*, comp. by Mary Wilder Tileston (Minneapolis, MN: World Wide Publications, 1986), July 29.

14. Elisabeth Elliot, *Finding You Way Through Loneliness* (Grand Rapids, MI: Revell, Baker Publishing Group, Spire Edition, 2011), 64.

15. Jon Courson, *Jon Courson's Application Commentary, New Testament* (Nashville, TN: Thomas Nelson, Inc., 2003), 1282.

16. Jon Courson, *Jon Courson's Application Commentary, Old Testament, Volume I: Genesis–Job* (Nashville, TN:Thomas Nelson, Inc., 2005), 1304-1305.

17. Charles H. Spurgeon, *Morning and Evening*, January 9, evening reading.

18. Hannah Hurnard, *Hinds' Feet on High Places, Children's Version,* arr. Dian Layton (Shippensburg, PA:Destiny Image Publishers, Inc., 1993), 57.

19. Ibid., 28

20. A.H. Francke, quoted in *Joy and Strength*, comp. Mary Wilder Tileston (Minneapolis, MN: World Wide Publications, 1986), September 20.

21. Charles H. Spurgeon, quoted in *Streams in the Desert*, comp. L.B. Cowman, updated by Jim Reimann (Grand Rapids, MI:Zondervan, 1997), September 22.

22. Hannah Hurnard, *Hinds' Feet on High Places, Children's Version,* arr. Dian Layton (Shippensburg, PA:Destiny Image Publishers, Inc. 1993), 96.

23. Jon Courson, Jon *Courson's Application Commentary, Old Testament, Volume II: Psalms–Malachi* (Nashville, TN:Thomas Nelson, Inc., 2006), 428.

24. A.C.A. Hall, quoted in *Joy and Strength*, comp. Mary Wilder Tileston (Minneapolis, MN: World Wide Publications, 1986), October 5.

25. Elisabeth Elliot, *Finding You Way Through Loneliness* (Grand Rapids, MI: Revell, Baker Publishing Group, Spire Edition, 2011), 51.

26. Ibid., 162, 163.

27. Frances J. Roberts, *Come Away My Beloved* (Uhrichsville, OH: Barbour

Publishing, Inc, 2002), 83-84.

28. Jon Courson, *Jon Courson's Application Commentary, Old Testament, Volume II: Psalms–Malachi* (Nashville, TN:Thomas Nelson, Inc., 2006), 552.

29. Elisabeth Elliot, *Finding You Way Through Loneliness* (Grand Rapids, MI: Revell, Baker Publishing Group, Spire Edition, 2011), 27.

30. Ibid., 26.

31. Francois Fenelon, *The Seeking Heart* (Sargent, GA: Christian Books Publishing House, 1992), 115.

32. Charles H. Spurgeon, *Morning and Evening*, November 11, evening reading.

33. Bethany Dorin, "Michael's Song," 2011.

34. *The Hiding Place*, directed by James. F Collier, (World Wide Pictures, 1975).

35. Jon Courson, *Jon Courson's Application Commentary, New Testament* (Nashville, TN: Thomas Nelson, Inc., 2003), 1545-1546.

36. F. B Meyer, *Our Daily Homily*, Psalm 148:8.

37. T. T. Carter, quoted in *Joy and Strength*, comp. Mary Wilder Tileston (Minneapolis, MN: World Wide Publications, 1986), December 28.

38. Annie Johnson Flint, quoted in *Streams in the Desert*, comp. L.B. Cowman, updated by Jim Reimann (Grand Rapids, MI: Zondervan, 1997), January 6.

39. Jon Courson, *Jon Courson's Application Commentary, New Testament* (Nashville, TN: Thomas Nelson, Inc., 2003), 1472.

40. Francois Fenelon, quoted in *Joy and Strength*, comp. Mary Wilder Tileston (Minneapolis, MN: World Wide Publications, 1986), January 21.

41. Charles H. Spurgeon, *Morning and Evening*, January 23, morning reading.

42. L. B. Cowman, *Streams in the Desert*, comp. L.B. Cowman, updated by Jim Reimann (Grand Rapids, MI:Zondervan, 1997), January 24.

43. Jon Courson, *Jon Courson's Application Commentary, Old Testament, Volume I: Genesis–Job* (Nashville, TN:Thomas Nelson, Inc., 2005), 428.

44. Edith Schaeffer, *Affliction* (Old Tappan, NJ:Fleming H. Revell Company, 1978), 159-160.

45. Austin Phelps, quoted in *Streams in the Desert*, comp. L.B. Cowman, updated by Jim Reimann (Grand Rapids, MI:Zondervan, 1997), December 2.

46. The Des Moines Sunday Register, Obituaries, Sunday, January 29, 2012, B4.

47. Benjamin Dorin, http://youngmenservinggod.blogspot.com/2012/01/hallmark-of-courage.html, accessed February 4, 2014.

48. J. R. Macduff, quoted in *Streams in the Desert*, comp. L.B. Cowman, updated by Jim Reimann (Grand Rapids, MI:Zondervan, 1997), February 6.

49. Nancy Leigh DeMoss, *Choosing Gratitude*, (Chicago, IL:Moody Publishers, 2009),17.

50. J. R. Miller, quoted in *Streams in the Desert*, comp. L.B. Cowman, updated by Jim Reimann (Grand Rapids, MI:Zondervan, 1997), March 11.

51. Paul E. Billheimer, *Don't Waste Your Sorrows*, (Minneapolis, MN: Bethany House Publishers, 2006), 80-81.

52. Ruth Meyers, *The Perfect Love*, (Colorado Springs, CO:Waterbrook Press, 1998), 101-102

53. Randy Alcorn, *Heaven* (Carol Stream, IL: Tyndale House Publishers, Inc., 2004), 471

Made in the USA
Lexington, KY
29 May 2017